Jesus Freak Buddha Geek

A Spiritual Journey And Memoir In Anecdote

T. L. Fitzgerald

Copyright page

JesusFreakBuddhaGeekbook.com

ISBN #: 979-8- 3304-5722-9

Imprint: Ingram Spark: Self-Publishing Book Company | Print & Distribute

https://www.ingramspark.com

(Paperback version.)

Front cover photography art by Zachary Fitzgerald.

Proofreading and mentoring by Michael, Hannah, and Zachary Fitzgerald, and Victoria Barnum; Unconditional, enthusiastic, and passionate support, belief, and encouragement by Michael, Hannah, and Zachary Fitzgerald, and Victoria Barnum.

Printed by Ingram Spark: Self-Publishing Book Company | Print & Distribute

https://www.ingramspark.com in

Dedication

For my husband who saved me —
and continues to save me — in every
way possible, and to our children.
We were born on the day that they
were born.

Table of Contents

Part I Author's note part I, prologue, and contemplate and meditate

Author's note part I

The intent and purpose of my background story is simply to share my own emotional growth and transformation, out of my own personal experiences (simply as I have remembered them), what brought me to the place that I am now, what I have learned, – (what I did with it – what I'm doing with it), and who I am now, because, and in spite of it.

In. no. way. whatsoever. is there any intent of 'malice' – rather, an intent to show hope to whoever needs to see it, that it is possible! to have the fortitude to get to a path that leads to a beautiful lifejourney filled with light, peace, safekeeping, and joy.

I hope you will, as I do, look on this story as a story of fortitude and strength; survival and release; peace, thrival, and steadfast safekeeping; and finally, humility and compassion in the midst of trauma. It needs to be a perfect mix! and balance of all parts – every part as important as the other! I want to share my journey, my joy, my outcome, my release, and my peace.

The following is not my life
story, but, stories from my life.

*"And thou shalt be secure,
because there is hope; yea, thou shalt dig
about thee, and thou shalt take thy rest in
safety"* [King James Version (KJV),
Job 11:18]

Prologue

I refound my need, my love and
devotion, for Jesus in my life, about
forty years ago. He, along with my
husband wcrc thc peace   the safe
place – that I felt I had been
missing and craving in my life up
until then. The peace and the safe
place, in exchange of isolation*;   in
exchange of indifference*,
absence*, and neglect*;   in
exchange of indignity*, violation*,
and trauma*;   in exchange of
dissociation;   in exchange of
chronic shame – self neglect, a
result;   in exchange of a need* for
hypervigilance – (the listening-for-
every-footstep kind);   and in
exchange of denial – the façade* –

that befell* most of my formative —
childhood — teen years, and even
beyond.

Repressed memory, A Savior.
Until it isn't.
The Remembering, now the
Protector.
Survival. "Thriv-al**"

Jesus, along with my
husband — and then the arrival of
our children, were the peace and the
safe place that forged my path to
freedom, focus, self-realization, and
to being able to fully live in the
present moment. A path to
awareness — of self-potential, self-
worth, and eventually self-care and
self-love. A path to breath. A
path to humility, and of caring and

doing for others. And a path to unshakeable strength and resolve. I flipped the page on my 'page-a-day' desk calendar this morning, to this quote: *"Our pain will inform us, but it doesn't have to define us"* (Sara Kuburic, 2024) – 'Millennial Therapist – Page-A-Day Calendar' Wow. And yes. And thank you. I had been struggling for so long to say the words, "I Did have (emotional) pain." I Do have emotional pain. However. – '(My) pain (can) INFORM (me) but it doesn't have to define (me)'. Yes. SO Good. It INFORMED me with the direction that I needed, to move forward – in order to attain the peace and safety that I so deeply needed and desired. Maya Angelou

(1928-2014) said, *"There's a place in you that you must keep inviolate "That may be the place where you go to when you meet God'* (2013)

This is my journey – my walk from hopeless to Hope.

I remember when I was newly married, in my early twenties (and at that time hadn't entertained the thought of church, or of having Jesus in my life, in many years), and I was standing in my mother-in-law's kitchen and noticed her wall calendar – (she had circled the date March 19th and wrote in: *"St. Joseph's Day"*). I asked her what St. Joseph's Day was and she said, "That's my guy***." That was one of my turning-point-moments, forming the trajectory of the spiritual path and journey I would be on. I researched St. Joseph's

Day and I became obsessed with learning about all of the Saints. There was a Catholic gift shop in my hometown that I would love to shop in for (*all the*) prayer cards – they even had greeting cards for the different 'Patron Saint' days. I felt reacquainted, reborn – awakened – to my love and need for Jesus in my life.

I needed a foundation – Jesus became my core[note 1] and my husband and our children became my mantle[note 2]

Almost fifteen years ago, again I had a pronounced – profound – spiritual shift (awakening) in my way of thinking. This was also at the time that Buddhist philosophy had gotten my attention, – and *Super Soul Sunday* had made its way into my living room. Soul food. Soul air. The thing about a spiritual journey is that we are always learning – always growing – always awakening – on the way to our own enlightenment, our illumination.

The days are past that I can think of a "religion" in terms of completely unquestioned beliefs, tenets, stories; – unconditional acceptance; – all as one absolute whole. But there is a definite spiritual hunger present, in these times we are living in, and I have it too. I take the parts – the beliefs – of different "religions" and philosophies, that I love, that I need, that I crave, that nourish me, that fill me up. Not requiring myself to blindly accept every single teaching (word) of any one "religion" or philosophy as my absolute – as a 'take-it-or-leave-it'. Can I be *Catholic*, and practice and love some of the parts of Buddhist philosophy, (and of other "religions" and philosophies, as well), at the same time? – and allow myself the freedom to reject what I need to reject? Different "religions" and philosophies compliment each other. Jesus' ministry gives messages of hope and healing and teaches faith and kindness and love; Buddhism has messages of compassion, kindness, love, and an end to suffering; to name but just a few of the overlapping philosophies that I love between these teachings and practices. Prayer. Manifestation. It doesn't have to be just one ("religion" or philosophy) or the other, in your life. This is a personal choice, personal to one's own perspectives and convictions. I absolutely need and love certain things from each table. There are things that I really don't believe in or like at all from each table. My path has become a beautiful, blessed, healing, concurrent path of contemplation and meditation. Prayer. Healing. Awareness. Mindfulness.

Call me a *cafeteria Catholic*. Call me a curious *Catholic*. What I know for sure is that I Do Need nourishment and comfort for my soul. This recipe works for me. It's not an all-or-

nothing Feast. Just some
food for thought.

note 1 and note 2 — one of the things
that a core and a mantle are
metaphors for, is the earth. The
core being the center and the
mantle being the next protective
layer. In the bible, a mantle is
literally defined as a cloak, and
one was specifically mentioned as
being wrapped around Jesus
completely. A core, in the bible, is
defined as the heart of something. I
think of a core as a foundation — as
roots — and a mantle as a place
where you are protected and safe.

Text annotations

*simply my own memories of

experiences.

**the act of thriving.

***('Takeaways for Sustenance'): I feel like a lot of us have 'their person' ('their' Saint) that they go to – (pray to). St. Anthony came to be 'my person' – 'my guy' – after I had prayed to him when I had lost something once (he is the 'Patron Saint for lost items'), and then he just became my (go-to) person (to pray to – to talk to). (I always feel an assuredness with him – he's unfailingly there for me.)

"Thy word is a lamp unto my feet, and a light unto my path" (Psalm 119:105)

Contemplate and Meditate

Contemplate

Lectio Divina (divine reading) has been a way of reading scriptures for centuries. This prayer practice is about pausing to reflect and pray, and being open to hearing what God wants to say to us. The steps of this practice are widely likened to feasting on the Word: the first taste (reading), chewing on it (meditating), savoring (praying), and digesting (contemplating). A spiritual feast. Soul food. Spirit nourishment.

Meditate

     Meditation is a practice
that is used in the Buddhist faith
and philosophy, to overcome
suffering, and to embark on the
path to inner peace and wisdom.
The Buddha sat under a rose-apple
tree ('the tree of enlightenment')
with the purpose of attaining deep
insight into suffering. Having
achieved this, he then set out
compassionately to show others the
path he had followed, so that their
lives might benefit and be touched
by his own insight and experience.

Preface

(Regarding the preceding,
this book offers a Contemplate
section and a Meditate section at
the beginning and end of each
chapter, respectively – in the spirit
of 'feasting on the word', and of
offering a taste of bible verse and of
both Jesus' ministry and Buddhist
philosophy. I hope it will feed your
soul.)

Part II Holding space: safe spaces and the people we hold space with

Soul snacks (memory morsels)

Part II is a collection of anecdotal essays, from both my childhood, and my adulthood: the safe spaces* – the reprieves* – that were my grandparents' houses; the ways that I have been blessed to have instances of holding space as an adult – (both of the above being examples of sacred in the ordinary, divine in the everyday); and the humility I feel, to have been given the gift of fortitude in difficult times and gratitude in joyous times. *"The LORD is my strength and song, and he is become my salvation."* (Exodus 15:2) Yes! He is both a strength and a song on my journey.

Text annotation

*simply my own feelings.

Breath of spiritual belonging —

safekeeping…

Chapter 1

Mady

Contemplate

*"If there be therefore any
consolation in Christ, if any comfort of
love, if any fellowship of the Spirit, if any
bowels* and mercies, Fulfil ye my joy, that
ye be likeminded, having the same love,
being of one accord, of one mind"*
(Philippians 2:1-2)

Text annotation

*Innate compassion; tender and
sympathetic emotions.

I can still picture my
paternal grandmother, Mady

(pronounced Moddy) and still feel
the feeling that I would have as I
would walk down the sidewalk and
up the steps to her door. She's
been gone from us – from this earth
– for more than three decades now,
but I can still see and hear her there
at the door, *crying out in just overt joy*
to greet all who would arrive
there. At the ready with the biggest,
softest, *rosiest scented* hug. This was
her greeting, every. time. I really
miss that.

    *(My husband's grandmother, our
Nonni, would sit on a chair near the door
at the entrance to my mother-in-law's
kitchen, and as you walked in, take your
face in her hands, kiss you repeatedly, and
tell you that she loves you. Pure. Real.
And like Mady, just overt joy and
emotion, in her happiness at seeing you.)*

● ● ●

35

And *I* am often
overwhelmed – *just washed over* with
emotion – by my feelings *for my own
children. (I clap. Whether they've spent
the night and are walking down the hall
in the morning, or are arriving at our front
door… – I clap. I wonder if this is in
part to Mady's or Nonni's imprint on
me.)*

Even at the maturity level
of the young ages that I was, in
these instances, these emotions –
this love – was not lost on me. I
still appreciate and draw from it to
this day. It meant and means so
much to me.

They made me feel like I
was the most important person in
those moments of time. I learned
about holding space, before I even
knew that term or would know the

importance of it.

I wish I had gotten to see Mady more – and know her more – as a kid, and I wish I had more years with her as an adult. I would've talked to her about Jesus and our mutual love for Him. I can only imagine her talks with Him, looking out onto 'her' lake outside her window – she loved Him so. I would've talked to her about our mutual love of writing, and our mutual love of – and belief in – a *full-out decorated house.*

For me, Mady's house was Goodness. Good-naturedness. Realness. Humility. Attentiveness. Comfort. Light. Safe.

On a sidenote about my rediscovery in later years of my need and love for God – for Jesus – and for spirituality, some books and television shows that helped (re-)ignite this passion in my life were the books, '*Looking for Mary (Or, the Blessed Mother and Me)*', by Beverly Donofrio and '*A Month Of Sundays: Searching For The Spirit And My Sister*', by Julie Mars; and *all aspects, programs, and shorts* from the television show *Super Soul Sunday*. I find myself needing and wanting to be immersed in this refound – and newly found – spirituality. It feels like belonging – peace – a tearful joy at times.

I've become an admirer, lover, and somewhat of a collector, of religious things – statues,

artifacts, prayer cards, angels –
religious souvenirs, knick-knacks –
religious ephemera in general. (I
have a lot of trouble resisting – and
have an especially strong affinity to
– angels and statues of Mary).

Another moment in time
that I remember, where I felt the
surge of love and emotion for God
– for Jesus – and for spirituality was
one Christmas Eve after attending
midnight Mass. After Mass, we
came outside to discover that snow
had coated the stone steps of the
church. 'Sparkly' – light as a feather
– "Christmas snow" floating down
under the glow of the streetlights. I
still remember breathing in the cold
air, feeling something *higher, bigger
than me,* profound, good, impactful,
epiphanic; feeling awe-filled,

peacefilled. The feeling that there is
nothing like His love.

I still feel Mady here with
me, on our parallel walk, along with
the glimpses of (our) yesterday –
*...pink Canada mints in a candy dish on
the side table in her living room;... cups of
ice cold sun tea;... the Irish blessing wall-
hanging, behind the formica kitchen
table;... bologna and mustard on toast;...
a sleepover that involved going out to eat at
Eddie's* (one of my favorite spots to
go out to eat, still, fifty years later –
I'm sure because it is one of my
Mady memories);... *our Christmas
dinners on 'her' lake in her later years –
Mady's famous baked beans with loads of
bacon and brown sugar;... the best ever
Christmas-decorated house;...* and when
I was young, the emotional
profundity of Mady having me

stand in front of her mirror, saying,
'*I am Beautiful*,' '*I love me*,' – an
unknowing gift that she gave me,
that sat in my memory until I would
unwrap and appreciate it many
decades later in life.

　　(*One of Mady's favorite things
was when she could sit and just take in
the beauty of her tree (her 'girl') all
'dressed' for her at Christmastime, and the
pretty wrapped gifts underneath.*)　Time
is full of these seemingly small and
fleeting moments, but they add up
to the biggest feelings.

Meditate

　　"*Love is a gift of one's innermost
soul to another so both can be whole*"
(Buddha Siddhartha Gautama)

Recommended reading: *'Looking for Mary: (Or, the Blessed Mother and Me)'*, Beverly Donofrio, 2001); *'A Month Of Sundays: Searching For The Spirit And My Sister'*, Julie Mars, (2005)
Recommended watching: *'Super Soul Sunday'* (2011-2021)

Something to chew on

What is *your* experience of holding space? What would you like it to be?

For my beloved Otisco grandparents,
aunts, and uncles...

Breath of grounding — earthing —

safekeeping…

Chapter 2
Grandma's and Grandpa's house

Contemplate

*"Children's children are
the crown of old (men)*;…"* (Proverbs
17:6)

*of the old

My maternal grandparents
had a house in (what I always
referred to, as) the country. As a
kid, it always felt like a long trip to
go visit them. (Funny, as an adult, I
now know that it wasn't a long trip
at all.)

There were only a few

houses on their street then… I
remember a big hilly yard that
wrapped around the front of their
house, lilac bushes, a chicken coop
in the backyard (that I was afraid to
go near), and an apple tree that I
used to love to climb – up, up, up.
The perfect climbing tree – so many
limbs – perfect for safeguarding.
Safekeeping.

My mantle.

———————————

There was a big garage far
over to the right, where my grandpa
used to work on old cars – Pete's
Garage. I remember the familiar
(garage) smell on Grandpa's green
work shirts – (and always his

• • •

trademark pocket protectors).

———————————

I can picture the view
beyond the edge of their backyard; a
vast farmer's field, and then down a
hill, sporadic farmhouses and a
quilt-like pattern of farmland.

———————————

Hot sticky summers; cloud-
watching on my back (what I have
now come to call *grounding* or
earthing); and the buzzing of insects
on the tall sticky grass all around
me… (my memory seems to always
go right to the hot sticky buggy
summers when reminiscing about

my childhood days spent at my
grandparents' house – both of my
grandparents' houses in fact).
Perfectly endless summer days.
Then cool reprieve inside the
farmhouse, the coolness of the dirt
cellar apparent (*and the delicious waft
of apples from the bushelfuls of apples –
from the local apple orchards – sitting in
the cellar*); going up the steps to the
'new living room' – quiet, walls
lined with windows and
bookshelves – the bookshelves
filled right up with books; a comfy
down-filled couch in the middle of
the room that you would sink into;
and the piano next to the doorway.
This room was usually off limits,
however, my extended cousins, a
year older than me, were allowed to
play the piano in there, and I, being

the oldest grandchild, may have
been a little spoiled, and was
allowed in there also – plus I was a
bookworm and I would be so
excited when Grandpa said I could
pick out a book to read while I sat
in there. This ended up being such
a gift that I would carry with me
forever – the quietude, thereby
inner peace; and an introduction to
my lifelong love of books.

There was a big tropical
fish tank in the family room on the
main floor that I loved to look at –
especially the fish that would 'kiss'
the side of the tank. My younger
aunt's, and my uncles' bedrooms
were upstairs at that time. One of
the memories I have, is of the time
that I was sitting in the family room
as a young kid, watching Saturday

cartoons, and one of my teenage uncles walked up the cellar stairs, past the family room where I was sitting, then up the stairs to his room, with a llama in tow. (*He worked odd jobs at local farms and asked for a llama as payment on that day, I heard later.*) He looked at me and made the '*shushing*' motion to me as he walked past. I think I just watched with big eyes. (There is no doubt that I told on him.)

My grandparents had some farm animals too – I remember ducks, chickens, roosters, and cows. My uncle (with the pet llama) also tried to show me how to milk a cow once. I didn't love it. And once, one of the roosters landed on my head, and proceeded to peck down at the ice cream cone I was holding.

It was terrifying. As I reminisce
about this, I am coming to the
conclusion that I loved my
grandparents' house as a kid, but
the farm animals, not so much.

———————————

My grandfather would
always say (an '*off the cuff*') prayer
before dinner. He always had
beautiful sentiments for all that he
was thankful for, including how
specifically thankful he was for
every single person sitting around
the table.

———————————

At night, it would get cold
in the house. There were all of the

creaks and moans and sounds that
an old farmhouse makes – and
outside, the loud night sounds of
the insects and farm animals, under
the thick wool blanket of night,
black as ink, covering the farm.
And there I would be, all bundled
up under a quilt, in the crisp cotton
sheets, in my teenage aunt's bed,
comfortable, content, Safe.

Although I *know* that no
person(s) is(are) perfect, I always
felt that the love and care given me
in that house, *was.* And I say the
same thing now to my own
children, that (*I know that I am far
from perfect – not "fishing" here – I know
I am not perfect. I've made mistakes and*

bad choices in my life, but) the love I
have for them is perfect.

Another very special
memory that I keep in my heart
from my grandparents' house is the
time that I spent the night when I
was little, and Grandma motioned
for me to open a certain cupboard,
and inside it were my favorite cereal
and juice waiting for me on the
shelf – *Froot Loops* and *Ocean Spray
cranberry juice cocktail.*

I have such a profound
appreciation for this act of love, one
of many. I think my days spent
there were probably some of my
first childhood experiences with just
Being Present – able and safe to just

be. And each moment I was in felt
eternal – in a good way – because
when you are able – and safe – to
just be fully present, it can make it
feel like the moment you are in lasts
longer. Safety, comfort, peace, and
time, all parts of one whole. Sitting
in this moment. Pieces of heaven
on earth. Pieces of peace. This
must be what eternal joy – eternal
life – feels like.

Meditate

Shanti Shanti Shanti (Sanskrit
term): peace three-fold: body,
mind, and spirit.

Yes.

Guardian angels

My grandparents were some
of our angels on earth; – and now
are our guardian angels along with
some of my aunts and uncles. I'm
sure our kids feel as though they
know them – they all very much live
on in our house through our stories
and memories of them – and
through their (and now our) family
traditions.

Something to chew on

When is an example of when you felt Safe to 'just *be*'? Do you have access to that place today and/or do you have an idea of a place where you could feel that way today? What do you remember about time spent at your grandparents' houses?

Holding space and safe
spaces…

Chapter 3
The cup of coffee

Contemplate

*"For I long to see you, that I
may impart unto you some spiritual gift, to
the end ye may be established*"*
(Romans 1:11)

Text annotation

*strengthened; loved.

    I am mostly an introvert.
And a self-proclaimed hermit. I
love alone time – peace. But once
someone comes over, the
dichotomous clingy part of me

takes over, and I am so distraught at
just the thought of them leaving.

What I like about a cup of
coffee is that the length of the visit
will at least last as long as the cup.

I find joy in the whole
process of brewing, smelling,
pouring (drinking) (the coffee).
Hands clasped around the cup —
savoring the heat, the first sip — *each
sip after, a reflective thought, — breath —*
an act of holding space with
another person. You face each
other on the couch, or on chairs
across the table. *Supports on a bridge.
Stable.* Fully sitting right here — in
This moment — talking with,
looking at, (studying their face,
watching them talk), bonding,
understanding, listening,

connecting with the person in front of you. All that matters. Everything else stops.

When someone holds space for you – with you, – is a listener, a sharer of your lifemoments, – it gives you a feeling of not only a record, proof, of your life and your story, but of proximity and belongingness. *"Ye are my witnesses, saith the LORD, and my servant whom I have chosen: that ye may know and believe me,…"* (Isaiah 43:10)

It's just pretty amazing to take the time to say *I see you,* really listen, and take the person(s) in fully – their aura, persona, soul, spirit, all in, and get to know them. To be here to listen and *to be their net* if needed. So beautiful, and surprisingly, a rare gift to receive.

• • •

Our most important human
condition. We're meant to connect.
It's how we heal. It's how we
thrive. It's beautiful and sacred. To
me, this is what holding space is.

You will have different
relationships with people
throughout your lifejourney. You
will need different people in your
life in the different seasons of your
life, and you will know who that is.
I have been out of school for over
forty years now [*I typed thirty at first,
thinking it was thirty, and then got out my
calculator – and… – (shaking my
head)…*]. The schoolmates that I
have reunited with, over social
media after all of these years, and
that I have a bond with now, are
not schoolmates I knew very well at
all while in school. I always say that

* * *

my circle is small, (*I'm a hermit, remember*), but I truly cherish the bonds I have made with these schoolmates, and it's so much better and different now, as an adult, – in this chapter of life.

I have different and specific relationships with different extended family members and the same with different coworkers. I cherish the uniqueness of each relationship – of each person. We are all (uniquely and) …*wonderfully made…(Psalm 139:14)* Holding space with someone – known or unknown to you – is humbling, and it is beautiful. And it is especially humbling to hear someone's story – *everyone. has. a. story.* – the rawness of their truth – fragile, breakable, requiring safekeeping.

* * *

I *hope* — *strive* — for our
house to feel so homey, welcoming,
and cozy that you feel as if you
never want to leave.

Finally, there is definitely
something to also be said for a first
cup of coffee in the morning
(alone). First sips in the early
morning, before the sun rises.
Reflection. Introspection. Quietude.
Gratitude. Perspective. Presence.
Plans.

Meditate

"True love is born from understanding"
(Buddha Siddhartha Gautama)

Something to chew on

       Who is your net? Who are
you a net for?

For Betty…

Mantles and normalcy…

Chapter 4

Two or more

Contemplate

"For where two or three are gathered together in my name, there am I in the midst of them" (Matthew 18:20)

Sometimes, holding space happens in a large group setting, such as a family dinner gathering. My husband comes from a large Italian family on his maternal side. I remember one dinner that we were invited to, at one of his extended cousin's houses. She has a very large immediate family of her own, and invited our family and our siblings' families, to a beautiful

homecooked dinner. I hardly have
the words to convey the beauty, the
love, the fellowship of this day and
the absolute giving of oneself –
next-level holding space – that was
shown to us all. We all sat down to
this incredible meal in her dining
room. I can practically smell it now
– stuffed veal roast, meatballs and
sausage in her homemade sauce… .
After dinner, we sat together and
looked at old family photographs
and reminisced together and learned
more about our common ancestors.
I am forever left with a beautiful
and humbled feeling about this day.
(Among other instances such as
this, this same extended cousin also
hosted all of us and even more
extended family as well – all were
welcome – for a Christmas dinner

at her house one year. She has the
biggest heart, truly selfless and
generous, and family is the most
important thing to her.)

And as time passes and as
we all get older, I also see this in my
own siblings (my in-laws, '*out-laws**')
– prioritizing time spent together.
It's beautiful. It is (an act that is)
never forgotten. Lives are busy.
Life has cycles. But then the
passage of time becomes an
epiphany – a powerful (and needed)
reminder of our *core... support...
certainty... constancy.*

———————————

Growing up, I would often
be at my maternal grandparents'
house for dinners where my

grandmother would make her spaghetti and meatball dinner with her homemade spaghetti sauce – (another core memory of my childhood if not the *most* core memory).

Their door was always open, and everyone was always welcome on 'spaghetti dinner day', as with any other day at their house. A note about this – this is another very special trait of my grandparents, as well as a sign of the times back then that doesn't happen at peoples' houses so much anymore: the open door – open house – hospitality. I think our own impression of our own so-called shortcomings of the states of our houses keeps people from doing this, as freely as in times past.

And we have such a yearning for it.
Holding space for each other is the
most important thing.

Grandma's sauce recipe
made enough to serve everyone
who walked in the door. I now
realize that sauce goes a long way,
but as a kid, it must have seemed
like a *magic never-ending kettle of sauce*!
It always felt like a special day. This
was a year-round tradition – a
celebration all on its own; the
familiar (amazing), distinctive smell
of Grandma's sauce hitting you in
the face when you walked in the
door; and everyone lining up at the
stove to get a scoop of angel hair
spaghetti covered in steaming hot
sauce. I think this was my
grandmother's greatest love
language – making her sauce for us

and opening her home to hold space for her family and friend-family. As far as my own love language, I think I inherited the former (I always say that I think feeding people is my love language!); I am working on the latter – (I am realizing that *as-is* is how you hold space with people).

My great-aunt and great-uncle (maternal side) are two more amazing examples of humility, of giving of oneself, and next-level holding space. They have a very large immediate family of their own, yet would make a meal at the ready for all and everyone who arrived at their kitchen door. I can remember an impromptu breakfast of eggs and bacon for several of us – nieces, nephews, great-nieces, great-

nephews, in the wee hours one
night when we showed up at their
door, following a family reunion
gathering that had run very late. (I
also have another core memory
with them from earlier in my
childhood when my brother and I
had spent the night there – they had
four children of their own at the
time, and they brought the whole
lot of us to a drive-in movie,
'Bedknobs And Broomsticks'. Before
we left for the movie, my great-aunt
made homemade sloppy joe
sandwiches for all of us, wrapped in
foil while they were hot, and
brought them out for us to enjoy at
the movie. I always say that *smells* =
memories and I can almost smell the
sloppy joes as I recall this. It's
something I never forgot about, –

have carried with me all of these years, – the giving of herself, the kindness and time, the feelings I felt that day of love and care, comfort, safety, happiness.

I have tried to pass down to the next generation – my own children – feelings such as these. I make my grandmother's sauce and meatballs recipe for each and every of their visits home, also wanting to pass down to them core memories made with love and care, that I was blessed to experience and know.

Meditate

"One moment can change a day
"One day can change a life and One life
can change the world' (Buddha Siddhartha Gautama)

*Out-laws — an affectionate term
my (*out-laws*) and I use for each
other — the spouses of our shared
mother-in-law's children. Our
own unique and special, cherished,
treasured, forever bond.

Something to chew on

    What is Your love
language? Who is your *core* and
your *support*? What is your *certainty*
and *constancy*?

For my in-laws, out-laws, and cousins-in-law...

For my in-laws, out-laws, and cousins-in-law...

Belonging – mantles and
normalcy…

Chapter 5
The table

Contemplate

"And they continued stedfastly
in the apostles' doctrine and fellowship,
and in breaking of bread, and in prayers
"And they, continuing daily with one
accord in the temple, and breaking bread*
from house to house, did eat their meat
with gladness and singleness of heart,"
(Acts 2:42 and 46)

Text annotation

*in agreement with.

The outside of our house

looks big. The inside is made up of very small spaces actually, due to the (unfortunate) layout of a raised-ranch style house. Our living room, dining room, and kitchen spaces are open to each other, in the shape of a narrow 'L' — (*the dining room and living room in one straight line, opposite a short kitchen, separated by a breakfast bar across the kitchen*).

I like a long table. At one of our largest dinner gatherings, (spaghetti dinner of course), we added a long collapsible table to our rectangular dining table. It took up the dining room plus most of the living room area. It made me so happy.

It's in the everyday stuff of life that you'll find the sacred — the authentic — and the vulnerable — in the sense of it simply being the act of being present and holding space, and not getting caught up in all the other details like a 'perfect space' in which to gather. Not just holding space – but simply sharing space – sharing the very air – in that moment in time. Imperfection is good and real and beautiful and rustic and raw and Comfort. Comfort of a shared history, tradition. Connection. Recognition. Belonging.

One of my favorite memories of my husband's grandmother, Nonni, is of sitting down for a family meal and when Nonni would spoon some parmesan cheese onto her sauce, if one of the ungrated pieces (the little chunks of cheese that inadvertently end up in a bag of fresh grated parmesan) ended up on her spoon,

I came from a large extended family, but a small immediate family. My husband came from a large extended family and also a large immediate family and I have now come to realize that large immediate families can be 'tricky'. But although we all have very different personalities, — and even though life and feelings with a big family can be tricky throughout the year — whenever we all gather together for a family meal, all of that stuff just falls away to the floor, upon greeting, replaced by a hug and family love. It continues to be a beautiful (and probably rare in

this day and age) constant, when we
reunite for a gathering together. As
your circle of people forms and
grows – and also changes
throughout your life, there really is a
(powerful) invisible cord – a cord
built of the act of holding space
together – that connects you, ties
your souls.

Illumination

        I do realize that, in spite of
the aforementioned, there are
Other Different situations or
scenarios in life where that is Not
going to be possible Nor should it
happen. (But also, on Another
note, can we also recognize the
times in life where it Is possible to

do it – to let the tricky stuff drop to the floor?)

As I've mentioned, I have my *hermit* side and my *peopley* side – and filling a long table with my people has the best of both worlds of being present and holding space. Sharing space. Sharing a meal. Breaking bread. Sitting across from, or next to, a loved one, – or a new acquaintance, – stopping, really seeing each other, being attentive. Time around you stops. And thereby, the magic of being present and holding space.

Another special moment in time at the table was one night when my immediate family were all home for dinner and we were at the table, eating and talking and laughing;— I got up to go get something from the kitchen;— and I had a realization, in the otherwise quiet of the kitchen just then, – that one of the best sounds I've ever heard was the sound I was hearing just then of *everyone's silverware 'clanking' against their plates.*

It symbolized much more to me than just the sound of the clanking silverware – it symbolized a moment together in time. A standing still. Sacred and cherished. It's good to just stop and take in the sounds and the moments once in awhile.

• • •

Meditate

*"He who experiences the unity of
life sees his own self in all beings"*
(Buddha Siddhartha Gautama)

My 'prize' (from the Italian-Greek
market where we buy the fresh
parmesan): a chunk of salty
locatelli, so good it should just be
called candy.

———————————

A *postscript* I'd like to insert:
my husband and I shared a day at
the lake this afternoon with some of
our siblings, in-laws, out-laws, … .
It was undoubtedly the most
beautiful day, weather-wise, of this
summer. We were having a

moment of remembrance for my
mother-in-law, who left this earth
and joined the angels twenty five
years ago – until we meet again.
Mom loved the water. We stood in
a circle with our arms around each
other and said a family prayer by the
water, and then we just soaked up
each others' company for the rest of
the day. There was a profundity to
this day I will keep with me. Good-
naturedness. Fellowship. Peace.
Familial love. Familial bond. We
ate, walked, talked, laughed, got
teary eyed. Raw, real, vulnerable,
safe. More 'sacred in the ordinary'.

Something to chew on

Do you feel comfortable today to hold space in your home 'as-is'? Do you know that holding space is about being with the people who are gathered – and not about the 'perfection' of the gathering *place?*

Spirit nourishment

Contemplate

Jesus' ministry is one of
compassion and kindness, of mercy
and love, of healing the broken and
the weak. The bible tells the story
of Ruth, who embodied courage
and sacrifice to stay with, and care,
for Naomi. She was then shown
blessings and happiness in her later
years as a result of her selfless and
kind actions.

Caregivers come in many
forms. And save us in many ways.
My own came in the form of many
different people, and the gifts I
received were that of time, and a
feeling of love, caring, safety, and
peace. Caregivers give of

themselves. Likewise, those who simply care About us and love us are giving of themselves to us too – (giving of oneself can also simply be the act of holding space for each other).

The moral of Ruth's story could be likened to the Buddhist principles of *Dharma* (a way of living life) and *Karma* (the sum of a persons' actions). Ruth was living her life with intention in this way simply from her own goodness, kindness, and love, and then would receive unbeknownst blessings in life.

"And the Levite, (because he hath no part nor inheritance with thee,) … shall eat and be satisfied; that the LORD thy God may bless thee in all the work of thine hand which thou doest"

(Deuteronomy 14:29)

(*You gave of yourself – asking…
expecting… nothing in return – and
God has blessed you for your good
works.)

Meditate

*"…A generous heart, kind
speech, and a life of service and compassion
are the things which renew humanity"*
(Buddha Siddhartha Gautama)

—————————

Buddhism promotes
nonattachment, however,
compassion and selflessness are still
core principles, and thought to be
key on the path to enlightenment.

The *Metta Sutta* consists of
three parts, likened to
bringing into being a great
tree from the time the seed
is sown, to the time the
tree is laden with fruit. The
first part is to show
loving-kindness, likened to
making one's life grow like
a tree. The second part is
to meditate loving-kindness,
resulting in one's entire life
becoming a source of joy.
The third part is the
commitment to showing
loving-kindness in all ways
to all: the spiritual love that
reflects the fruition of this
process. (Buddharakkhita,
1995)

Part III Rooted: all is connected

to all

Soul snacks (memory morsels)

Part III is a collection of anecdotal essays about our roots – both in nature and ancestry, and the amazement and wonder! – the comfort – in the knowledge – the epiphany – that all is connected to all! *"For thou art great, and doest wondrous things: Thou art God alone"* (Psalm 86:10)

Insight…

Chapter 6
Still waters

Contemplate

> *"He maketh* me to lie down in green pastures: he leadeth me beside the still waters"* (Psalm 23:2)

Text annotation

*Guides (sheep) to green pastures for food and rest.

Another *dichotomous trait* I have, is my relationship with bodies of water. On the one hand, I am very drawn to water – lakes, rivers, oceans, … swimming pools. On the other hand, I have a fear of

being in deep water, even from the
inside of a boat. But on the '*other
other*' hand, my favorite movie is
Jaws and I will watch it repeatedly –
I *have* watched it repeatedly. I'm
drawn to any television show
having anything to do with oceans,
whales, sharks … (*I'll be darned if I
know what's wrong with me.*) I just like
the close proximity of water to
myself … from land. *Or tv.*

———————————

At the end of a day spent at
our favorite (local) lake, the
sunlight will just rest on top of the
water right before sunset, – the light
flickering off of a million diamonds
on top of the blackness, – and these
are times that I look out and can

just *soak up the light into all of my senses, right to my soul,* and everything feels so right with the world. The connection to nature is so undeniable.

We all have a need to connect and (a) need for a place of calm and peace within ourself – (the latter resulting in a need for a spiritual space). A spiritual space may simply be in nature, it may simply be the comforting feeling of tradition, or it may be a moment of peace and quiet. A spiritual space has a healing impact. A longing to reach toward something higher and bigger than ourself is a human need, not limited to religious spaces. (Lassila, 2021)

Along with my attraction to
water, I've realized in my later years
that my attraction to trees and
mountains is even greater!   What a
grand metaphor though! – water
symbolizing the circle of life
through constancy. movement.
cleansing. rebirth. light. (Jesus and
my reconnection and love for him);
and then the connection I feel to
trees – *my "church"* – and mountains
– the importance in my life and the
longing for spaces for meditation
and reflection. (My inner buddha.)
(Me being dichotomous again.)

And one of the greatest
religious spaces of all, must be to
stand in front of any vista –
mountain range – row of trees –
body of water – and feel

simultaneously so small while in the presence of awe.

Meditate

    *"Learn this from water: loud splashes the brook(,) but the oceans(') depth(s) are calm"** (Buddha Siddhārtha Gautama)

Text annotation

*In regard to the complex nature and emotional states that are associated with water. (Once we are able 'to get out of our own head', all of the elements and qualities of something are then able to become clear.)

Something to chew on

      What do you feel
dichotomous about? Do you have a
spiritual space? – what types of
spaces are you drawn to for
quietude? – peace? – introspection?
– reflection?

For Cece, Matthew C., Mark R., Aunt

Phyllis and Krystal C....

Insight…

Chapter 7
Trees are church

Contemplate

"But all things that are reproved are made manifest by the light: for whatsoever doth make manifest is light" (Ephesians 5:13)

Text annotation

*The transformative power of light symbolizes divine guidance, understanding, revelation, as the light of Christ brings clarity. Epiphany. Light signifies the presence of God, and reveals His truth, through the Holy Spirit. The truth being spiritual illumination and enlightenment. *("What does Ephesians 5:13 mean?" bible.art. https://bible.art/meaning/ephesians-5:13)*

Sometimes, the littlest things – the *ordinariest* things – can be day-changing.

Looking up at the branches and the leaves against patches of blue sky have a profound. clarifying. joy-filled. impact on my mind, on my heart, and on my soul.

Luminous light pointedly lands on the branches, and shimmers and sparkles on the leaves, as flashes of periwinkle blue peek in between. Life-giving, epiphany-prompting, enlightenment-experiencing, moments of reflection and

gratitude. It makes me feel
connected to all – that all is well
with all. Well-being. Hope. Peace
falls over me, sunlight catches my
eye and fills me up inside! It's one
of my favorite things – one of my
favorite feelings, favorite times of
day. Inner peace is so profound, so
important; not only for your soul,
but your body, all of your inner self,
your organs…; it surfaces, shows on
your face; glows on your face from
within. Life-giving. You know that
feeling?... when you feel washed
over, filled up, with awe, well-being,
joy? My definition of that inner
peace is God.

I do have less energy these
days, am less mobile, – (our bodies
start to change – to seemingly
'betray' us as we get older) – am out

of breath quicker, — but as we
witness these moments of profound
beauty in nature, the feelings of
hope and possibility feel endless!
So many ways to be awake and
present. So many occasions to say
Thank You.

————————————

      Sitting at a stoplight in my
car, and glancing out the side
window, noticing the tall grass on
the side of the road — or
wildflowers, as if for the first
time... Feeling the warmth of the
sun... Smelling the warmth of the
sun... Taking in the beauty of all of
the trees or hills in your sight. They
can stop you and leave you
breathless, in awe. In every

season... In the depths of summer, dense and tall thickets of green line the sides of the road on either side of you like a HUG... In the peak of Fall they line up for you, *parade spectators, greeting you in their full glory of color...* And finally, the scatterings – the canopies – of yellow – envelop – like a hint to November's warmth of spirit that awaits.

I remember once on a drive home from work, when I really took in – really noticed and appreciated – the beauty of the trees in late Fall, long after the peak leaf-changing season here had ended – the trees covering the hills, looking *soft and grey and fuzzy in the distance.*

There's magic in looking over and noticing and "breathing in" a hill covered in trees, *but in summer — the fluidity of green!*

Mesmerizing.

Awe-inspiring.

Mood-altering.

Life-giving.

Epiphany-prompting.

(Nature moves me very deeply**.)

One summer day, I was waiting – sitting in my car in my husband's work parking lot – to pick him up after work. I looked over and caught sight of a long row of very tall trees, *shimmery, their leaves catching the sunlight,* touching the blue sky. That was the day that I told myself that *trees are church.* It was an overwhelming feeling – of beauty and awe and of *something higher – something bigger – something more than me.*

———————

We try to make the trip up
to the Adirondacks every year. As
soon as we enter Adirondack Park,
even if I hadn't seen the sign, I
would know that we had arrived.
You can see the change in trees –
the Adirondack trees – the change
in landscape; feel the change in the
very air – the coolness; smell the
delicious pine smell.

*(Maybe my soft spot for trees all
started with the safety of my grandparents'
tree.)*

———————

Sunrises and sunsets are
also (ordinary extraordinary) parts

of every day that really have an
effect on me. When I see a sunrise
on a clear morning, or the
distinctive sunsets that each season
holds and gifts to us, I always
reflexively say WOW – or
something along those lines, – out
loud – (as if no matter how many
times I've seen it, I still can't believe
it!). There's something in the
miraculous, seeing the sun rise. The
beauty and awe of it is worth getting
up, to be a witness to,… as many of
them as our life holds.

I was sitting on the steps on
our back deck today and heard what
I thought was a dog from another
yard. It was a single duck flying

right overhead – giving me pause –
memorable, striking, beautiful, in
spite of the *ordinariness* of it.
Sometimes the birds in our yard will
land, and rest, very close to where I
am sitting. The beauty and awe and
profundity of these kinds of
moments makes me feel so
humbled,– in just the same way as
the sight of a larger than life
creature like a crow or hawk flying
overhead.

———————————

You could say it is a gift?
that my circumstance – my own
unique lifejourney – would bring
me to appreciate life's (simple,
beautiful, ordinary) moments such
as these and this life that I now

have, with such appreciation, awe,
humility, and gratitude.

Text annotation

**common trait of highly
sensitive people.

Meditate

>   *"If we could see the miracle of a
single flower clearly, our whole life would
change"* (Buddha Siddhartha
Gautama)

Something to chew on

What feels like *church* to
You?

Faith…

Chapter 8

Thin places

or

the 'Christian fantasy' chapter?

or

the 'crossworlds fantasy' chapter?

(…it's totally up to you)

Contemplate

"And, behold, the veil of the temple was rent in twain from the top to the bottom; and the earth did quake, and the rocks rent;"* (Matthew 27:51)

(*In both a spiritual and literal sense, the barrier between men and God was removed by God.)

I have read that the

Celtic Saints have often referred to
somewhere as a *'thin place'*. I also
believe and feel that there are
certain times and places where the
veil between the spiritual and
material world is undeniably very
thin; as if 'a *degree away*'; like, that
place where you're *here* – but you
feel like you've touched on *there* –
the feeling of it brushing gently by
you.

The palpability of '*the thin
places*' is very present at solemn or
melancholy moments, especially
when thinking about or mourning
the loss of a loved one. And not
surprisingly, the times that I have
felt this most have been at funeral
services or cemeteries.

Feeling is seeing. Feeling is
being-with. (Even in the physical

world alone, you can palpably reach out and touch it – physically feel it in your throat or your gut – when your children – or any of your loved ones – are going through a difficult or painful time.) Sometimes, I get what I call '*signs*' – (mine usually come by way of music). I always stop, look up, and say, "*Oh, hello.*"

And I don't believe signs are ever coincidental. I believe we read something or see something or hear a particular song or stumble across something on the television or social media – at just the right time, the exact right moment, right when we need to, – to give us an epiphany or clarification. Synchronicity. To teach us, or show us something relevant to the moment or thought we are in, or to

give us a Hello at a particular
moment. (The Hellos 'come across
loud and clear'.)

A few months after my
maternal grandmother died, some
of her children, grandchildren, and
nieces and nephews were sitting at
the table at my grandparents' house
on Christmas Day, and one of my
younger uncles just started very
softly and sweetly singing a
Christmas carol, out of the blue.
(My grandmother loved Christmas.)
Everyone then joined in. It was a
very solemn, sacred, and beautiful
moment. Afterwards, someone else
started a song. We did this for a
while that afternoon. That day has
always stuck with me. I felt her
there that day.

I do believe that our loved

ones who have passed on are always
with us, guiding us, watching over
us, just as Jesus is and Saints are… .

Some of my family
members and I were in a car
accident a little over ten years ago. –
(We were ok from it.) We were hit
from behind and the point I'm
trying to arrive at, is that I do not
have a memory of the feeling or the
chaos of moving the car across the
other (oncoming) lane into a yard to
get out of harm's way. Rather it felt
something like being *'placed in the
palm of a hand and') gently placed down.*
I actually still remember that feeling
of peace and safety. *"Fear thou not;
for I am with thee: be not dismayed; for I
am thy God: I will strengthen thee; yea, I
will help thee; yea, I will uphold thee with
the right hand of my righteousness"*

(Isaiah 41:10)

In my own mind — *and yes also of my right mind,* — I actually have what is my own idea of heaven. I realize that probably very few people think of it in exactly the same way. Because truth be known, no-one knows; — we won't know until we're there. So I guess (it's obvious to say, that) you need to think of it in whatever way you need to think of it.

Having faith is a Choice we have… (*Lazarus.*)

I like the *thought* that (after we die) we will be able to be with the energy of our loved ones on earth at certain times (where the veil

is thin, let's say) – and that our
loved ones on earth may feel *us* –
(who have passed) – when everything
is in "that perfect alignment" as
well; that we would all have our
'own version' or impression* of
heaven. Meaning, our heaven is
what we need it to be – (and that
'our own 'details' can also be
duplicated into other peoples'
versions of their own heaven,
simultaneously'). (*Impression* –
(noun) – Oxford English Dictionary
(1857) Powered by Oxford Languages
https://languages.oup.com/google-
dictionary-en/ – *an idea, feeling, or*
opinion about something or someone,
especially one formed without conscious
thought or on the basis of little evidence.)

I believe that heaven is an
energy – and I like the *idea* or the

thought (the *Hope*) that *I* have, that we will be with our people and our animals (their energies) that we need to be with, and that we need to have around us; that we will be in the environments that we need to be in; the events or points in time – (as we knew time to be on earth); the perception of age that we need to think of ourselves in and that we need our people and our animals (their energies) to be. Very "*The Shack*" meets "*The Lovely Bones*", I know, (*sans* the heartbreak and horrificness).

Meditate

"Truth is hidden by the golden veil of the mundane. Pierce through this thin glittering sheath and know that you

are the Sun" (Sri Sri Ravi Shankar,
"Celebrating Silence", p.10, Arktos,
2014)

Guardian angels

Too many to list. I see you.
Some of you quite often.

Something to chew on

        Have you had an experience
of a 'thin place'?

For Kathleen Jeanette P.–C. and Robert A. and all of the generations of women before you, and Great-Aunt Ruth (my birthday buddy) and Nina Belle D.–M. and all of the generations of women before you...

Identity and belonging…

Chapter 9

Ancestor mine

Contemplate

"Now faith is the substance of things hoped for, the evidence of things not seen" (Hebrews 11:1)

I have gone *up the ancestry tree*, taken a break from it, and am interested in climbing back up again. I don't know a lot about most of my grandparents – I Knew them, but not too much about their history or their ancestors' histories. So I am hungry for knowledge and revelations. I have already fallen in love with a few 'newly discovered' ancestors in reading their life stories through their obituaries.

My maternal grandparents had four young children when my (blood-relation) maternal grandfather tragically died. My grandmother met and married my (now) grandfather, he adopted her four children and they then had four more children. My (now) grandfather – who I have always known to be my grandfather – was Swedish, and I was a teenager when I found out that I wasn't (really) Swedish. Although, as an adult, I will now tell you that I am Swedish in my heart, have spent my entire sixty years celebrating my grandfather's Swedish heritage and traditions, and therefore AM pretty much Swedish.) It just wasn't talked about – at all – (in those days), as with so many other taboo topics. For this reason, I know basically nothing about my (blood-relation) maternal grandfather. I have one photo of him and one memory relating to him: once, my brother and I went along on a car ride with some family members (to visit) – *who I believe to have been* – a relative of my (blood-relation) maternal grandfather. I was very young, so it is a very vague memory. All I remember about that day was a winding road leading up a hill (to our destination), meeting a middle-aged woman there, and there being a *molasses-spice* smell in her house – of the cookies she had baked for us. That's the extent of it. I don't know how she was related. It was

never talked about again. It was a
little irrational the way this was a
taboo subject. I know the purpose
was to not hurt my grandfather's
feelings? – (as I said, the only
grandfather I knew to be my
maternal grandfather) – so the
decision was made to live around
(the reality – or truth – of) it. I
didn't hear anything about it again
until I was a teenager. And I found
out within the last twenty years that
my (blood-relation) maternal great-
grandfather was living until the
1970's, and once again, I had no
idea about that, and apparently a
decision was made* – (also
irrational) – for me, us, to not be
part of his life or know or get to
meet him. I feel like we can't
entirely know ourselves until we

know where/who we come from
and that most of us are hungry to
learn more about who we are,
especially as we get older. To know
the person better, whose facial
features or other traits we may see
in ourself?

My husband and I were
discussing my (blood-relation)
maternal grandfather once, and how
I wanted to learn about him, and
later that day my daughter and I
went for a walk – she was quite
young, like elementary school age –
and she must have overheard our
conversation and very matter-of-
factly turned to me and asked, "*So
who is 'so-and-so' anyway?*" And I told
her. Simple enough, right? She
said, "*Oh, okay.*"

And that was that.

My daughter is very matter-of-fact like that. I love it. It's how we communicate. My son is full of curiosity – he has a thirst for (and retainment of) knowledge of everything and anything under the sun. I love that too. They are the *smartest, most amazing, most beautiful humans I am privileged to know, and humbled and blessed to get to be a mom to.*

I recently met with an extended cousin on my paternal side. She is from another state and was here visiting her aunt and uncle and cousins. Her grandmother and my paternal grandmother were sisters. (My grandmother had three sisters in total.) I called my grandmother Mady (pronounced Moddy) and I learned on this visit for the first time that my cousin called her grandmother (my grandmother's sister) Mady, too! This was mind-blowing to me. Only because I never knew it! (Another interesting note is that this cousin is a writer, as is her sister, and also another of their immediate cousins. Their father was an author, also, and my grandmother also wrote many beautiful poems for us over the years.) I believe more and more, that traits (not only physical, but also emotional), strengths, abilities, interests, and even inclinations are truly inherited in a very straightforward way.

A note about this age we
live in with social media: the best
part – of course – are the
connections, and also the re-
connections. Re-connections to
childhood neighbors and friends,
and relatives who you don't have
the occasion to see anymore, and
haven't seen in a long time, – and
then connections to relatives in the
family tree that you had never met
or known about previously. I can
say that not only have I made
beautiful new bonds with old
friends and acquaintances in this
way but I have also been so blessed
to make brand new familial bonds.
The roots of our trees are our
origin, our past. If we care about –

and for – the roots, they can bring
life to the branches.

All is connected.

Meditate

"A jug fills drop by drop"
(Buddha Siddhartha Gautama)

Guardian angel

I mentioned falling in love
with 'newly discovered' ancestors
after reading their life stories
through their beautiful obituaries.
One of them, a distant ancestral
relative (distant cousin) on my

maternal's blood-related paternal side
named Kathleen, really resonated
with my soul – she had a love of
writing and belonged to a writing
group (local to where I live!), had a
passion for caring for elderly, and
was active in her church and in
women's groups. I am also
passionate about every one of these
things! I am truly in awe of the way
in which we are connected to our
ancestors, not just on the family
tree, but spiritually and emotionally.

Text annotation

*In my own opinion.

Something to chew on

Is there an ancestor you
would like to learn about?

Spirit nourishment

Contemplate

The roots of a tree absorb
nutrients and water for the
tree to live and thrive. As
humans, we are also rooted.
Our souls – and the roots
of our souls – are nourished
with God's love and with
the love of the people that
we connect with. All of life
needs – and flourishes in –
connectedness. (Ortberg,
2024)

*"I am the vine; you are the
branches."* (John 15:5)

Jesus Is the tree of life.

Meditate

All (of) life is

interconnected. All things
are mutually supporting,
and interrelated, forming
the whole. (Mahayana
Buddhism concept) We are
all a part of a larger fabric
of synchronicity. We are all
connected to all. (Ikeda
Sensei, 2024)

Part IV Core and mantle: a foundation and a safe place

Soul snacks (memory morsels)

Part IV is another collection of anecdotal essays from my childhood and my adulthood, and also motherhood and our childrens' childhood. And the humble reminder to myself that not only was I given the fortitude to walk on a path that culminated in a lifejourney where I now have a core* and a mantle*, but also – and even moreso – a gift of being able to be a core and a mantle for our own children, the gift and the joy of motherhood, and how very humbled! and lucky I feel to have been given these gifts in life. "*As one whom his mother comforteth, so will I comfort you;…*" (Isaiah 66:13)

*foundation, roots; and *safe place
— "protective layer".

*For my **Angel** and
my **Star**...*

Core and mantle – salvation

– a life transformed – the

future and the reason – love

and family – and the heart*

of my all…

(* " 'Heart' occurs over one
thousand times in the Bible, making
it the most common
anthropological term in the
Scripture."
https://www.biblestudytools.com/
dictionaries/bakers-evangelical-
dictionary/heart.html "In the
Bible, the heart is considered the
seat of life or strength. Hence, it
means mind, soul, spirit, or one's
entire emotional nature and
understanding." Creation Science 2
of 9 - California State University,

Northridge, 'DOES THE BIBLE
CONTRADICT ACCEPTED
BIOLOGICAL CONCEPTS?',
Lorence G. Collins
https://www.csun.edu/~vcgeo005
/heart.html#:~:text=In%20the%20
Bible%20the%20heart,entire%20em
otional%20nature%20and%20under
standing)

Chapter 10

Joyful, joyful

Contemplate

*"Rejoice in the Lord always: and
again I say, Rejoice"* (Philippians 4:4)

When the time came that I
would be a Mom, I was 100% ready
for it. I was older than some new
Moms I knew, (I was thirty-one)
but I was really ready, and I don't
know that I really was before that,
even though ironically we had been
hoping for it for many years… *God
is always on time... (Ecclesiastes 3:11)*
And then we were blessed with two
at once.

One of each. One of the MANY

gifts this has given me as a mom is
the realization over the years that
you will never have a best friend
like your girl, and no-one will ever
love you like your boy. They are
our whole heart – and our whole
world. All the minutes in every year
holds new gifts with them and every
day we are with them is our favorite
day.

My mother-in-law and her
best friend both have twins. They
met at a twins' club. My husband
(not a twin) and I hoped to have a
baby for many years before it finally
came to be. And when it did, it
took us awhile to believe that it was
real. I remember when my doctor
was sitting at his desk across from
me in his office, when we had
officially found out that we were

expecting. I said, "*I don't believe it,*"
and he smiled and said, "*Neither do
I,*" and came around to where I was
sitting and kissed me on the
forehead.

Then we found out about
four months later that there were
two. Mostly I remember the feeling
during all of that time as being
nervous between each sonogram,
but overall, walking around in a
state of just joy. Planning and
thinking and strategizing and
smiling and realizing and crying and
laughing… really no words
sufficient to describe it.

I had been taken out of
work earlier than normal as a
precautionary measure and was on
'modified bed rest' – meaning, I was
allowed to sit on the couch, and get

up to go to the bathroom, or get something quick from the kitchen. My husband was at ranger college in the Adirondacks and came home every Friday afternoon for the weekend. At eight months, my mother-in-law and her best friend (*the OG twin moms*) took me to see a movie to get me out of the house – '*Bridges Of Madison County*'. It was carefully planned out – I was picked up and dropped off everywhere I needed to be that afternoon – minimal walking. We stopped for an ice cream in the mall next to the theater, and a woman looked at my belly and said, "*How many?*" My mother-in-law and her best friend jokingly referred to our row in the theater as '*reserved for the twin moms*' to everyone passing by.

At the end of the movie
they brought me home – (*sidenote – I
had been visiting the restroom a lot during
the movie, and my mother-in-law's best
friend sensed something was up that
night*). In light of that, my mother-
in-law offered to stay the night, but
I insisted, "*No, that's ok* "*I'm going to
get some sleep and Mike will be home
tomorrow*"… I made a "snack" (of
macaroni and butter) later that
night, my husband called as he did
every night, I said, "*Nothing going on
here* "*Dr. Klein said everything looks good
and on schedule* (at my dr. appt. the
previous day) "*He said he will see us in
four weeks* "*All is well, see you
tomorrow,*" and I would be woken up
in the middle of the night that night
by our golden retriever who seemed
to know that my water had broken.

And it had.

Timing.

(Some background – my husband's campus was in the Adirondacks. He had made friends with local bar-restaurant owners nearby the campus, husband and wife, and had told them our story. Since both the campus and the restaurant were kind of in the middle of the wilderness up there, they gave him their phone number on a matchbook 'just in case' to give to me, in case I couldn't reach him.)

The night my water broke, he had just gone to bed after working all day and studying into the wee hours – and this was before cell phones were the norm so there was just a pay phone in the dorm hallway. I tried calling it of course and it rang and rang. Everyone was

sleeping. He had my doctor's
phone number and the ambulance's
phone number programmed into
our home phone for me, and I
called my doctor next — (at two or
three in the morning). He was so
calming and told me to call the
ambulance and he'd meet me at the
hospital, and to try my husband
again. I still couldn't get through
on the dorm phone, so reluctantly I
opened up THE matchbook, called
the number in it, a woman
answered and immediately said, "*Is
this Terry? I'm on my way hon — I'll go
get him.*" When she got to his
doorway in the dorm building, she
said, "*Is there a daddy of twins here?*"
(The dorm building was normally
locked, but the door was open that
night. Guardian angels

everywhere.)

Before the ambulance came, I was standing in the living room, I put my hand on my belly, and said through happy and nervous tears, *"I'm going to meet you tonight"* – (I'd have to say, *THE* best moment in my whole life, next to actually meeting them). (I had an empty suitcase on the floor next to me that I in fact would bring with me that night because, well, I wasn't thinking straight)… And my mind had also gone completely blank as far as calling any other person on the planet that I might know, for help that night. Once I was in the ambulance, it dawned on me to call my mother-in-law, and she met me at the emergency room door as I heard her familiar voice say, *"Nana here"* My doctor had determined that a C-section would be the plan and asked what time I thought my husband would arrive. I thought three hours but I'm pretty sure he made it there in much less time. When he got there, he was hurriedly trying to find the room and was dropping his stuff in the hall and the nurses were picking it up behind him.... When he arrived at the room, my mother-in-law and I were just hanging out, talking, laughing, waiting for him and for the scheduled C-section – (and of course I was *'made comfortable' at that time*)... Catching his breath, he said, "*Aren't you supposed to be doing something?*"

Our neighbors across the street worked odd hours at a

penitentiary. I found out later, that
when the husband got home from
work, the wife said, "*I think she might
have gone tonight.*" (Because an
ambulance, a fire squad car, and
two police cars had come when I
called the ambulance.)

We were/are so amazingly
lucky in every way. To be blessed
with babies – and then the way
everything aligned and worked out
that night – (two) one month
premature but very healthy babies –
and to be able to walk on our
journey through life together with
these two beautiful and amazing
human beings – with more love and
pride and gratitude than words
could ever express, our hearts to
bursting. *I remember well how all of
those days felt. I remember how they*

*smelled... and how they felt,... picking
them up from their cribs and carrying them
into the living room each day... I
remember their faces... and how much
love and care I felt inside;... how much I
loved to care for them;... and now how
much I love them and love to care for
them;... how much I love everything they
say, everything they do... — everyday,... —
everything we do together,... big,...
small;... every moment spent together,...
or from afar... I'm obviously having
trouble putting the feelings into words —
because there aren't words to contain how I
— and we — feel about them.*

(Another double blessing I
had were my step-mother-in-law,
and my father-in-law, who stayed
nights with me and helped me, until
my husband would be permanently
home in the following weeks!) And

those special – forever –
grandparent bonds (like I cherished
with my own) were made in those
weeks.

Our kids are our best
friends. I try to be a better mom
each and every day – each and every
year – because it's my most
important job and also because
they're our most important people,
the loves of our lives, our smiles,
our world! As I've said, I know that
I am not perfect. But my love for
them is perfect. We are so very
lucky and so very blessed!

Wherever your path leads
to in this life or whatever path you
choose, I think that a common
thread that we all share is that our
own joy fully correlates to (the love
that we carry and) the love and care

that we give to others.

Meditate

   "Your purpose in life is to find your purpose and give your whole heart and soul to it" (Siddhartha Gautama Buddha)

   Yes.

____

Guardian angel

   I wish Nana had had a lot more years on earth with us. I'm grateful she was here with us to greet the twins the morning they came into our world, and to spend their first four years making many memories with them that they still talk about. I know she watches and guides and protects us still now every day. She will always live in us and through us and is part of our life and our traditions every day.

Angels on earth

I don't know what I would've done without my step-mother-in-law and my father-in-law in those first weeks that I was home alone with the twins — and quite honestly ofttimes! ever since then. Some of our guardian angels/ safeguarders/ safekeepers walk with us side-by-side here on earth. And if you're very lucky like us, they are your childrens' grandparents and two of their forever best friends.

I'm a mom of twins. *Every
time I say it – every time I think about it
– realize it, – it makes me feel happy.*

Something to chew on

What/who do you love?

What brings you joy?

For Uncle Roger…

Tradition of yore…

Chapter 11

Thanksgiving of yore

Contemplate

"Be not forgetful to entertain strangers: for thereby some have entertained angels unawares" (Hebrews 13:2)

Thanksgiving mornings are another of my core childhood memories. We would get up before dawn, and my little brother and I would be in the car with a coat right over our pajamas, ready to travel to our maternal grandparents' house. "Over the river and through the woods" — or at least that's what it

always brought to mind. (Those
were the years when the snow in the
yard was thigh-high here, well
before Thanksgiving.) The reason
for the early wake-up call was
because my grandmother hosted
Thanksgiving – an *all-day-revolving-
door-open-house* – with some of the
families of her nine siblings, and the
families of her eight children. We
would arrive early so that we could
help with the preparations and the
cooking. The food would be set
out buffet-style and any and all were
welcome to come and eat and visit,
at any time during the day.
Everyone would just sit anywhere
there was room. Chairs at the table,
or by the wood stove, stools at the
breakfast counter, on the stair steps,
and on picnic benches and lawn

chairs that were brought into the
house. Some would stand and eat.
All that mattered was that we were
all together in the same room.
Holding space together, if only for
that one day of the year for some.

      When we would first arrive,
my brother and I would go find
places to go back to sleep for
awhile. And then when we were up
again, we would go sit on the stools
at the breakfast counter to start
chopping up gumdrops with a
plastic knife, for the gumdrop
cookies. The breakfast counter
would already be full of my
grandmother's pies that she had
been busy baking up to that day –
blueberry, cherry, pumpkin,
mincemeat, and her fruitcakes.
Many years later, (when these

gatherings at my grandparents'
house would be but only memories
tucked safely away in our hearts and
minds), my husband and I would be
hosting a family gathering in our
first house, and I was beautifully
reminded again of the
unimportance of the size of a space
when having a family gathering.
One of my husband's uncles said to
me, "*It doesn't matter how big or small
your house is* "It's about the people in it,"
when I apologized for how small
our house was. I never forgot that,
and it is so true. The profundity
and beauty of that statement really
hit me. It always stuck with me and
changed my way of thinking about
what's really important at a
gathering. It's not about how big or
beautiful or perfect the house is.

It's about your people. Your circle.
And holding space with them.

We also traveled to this
same grandparents' house on
Christmas morning. A few of the
memories that I have of their house
on that day that really stick out to
me are my grandfather's Swedish
glögg warming in a tall kettle on the
stove, infusing the room; the
Swedish Christmas music playing
(which remains one of our own
special traditions now); the menu of
Swedish meatballs*, ham, and
scalloped potatoes (also our own
traditional Christmas meal still); and
the fact that Christmas day was also
my grandpa's birthday which I
always thought was really cool.

Text annotation

*Our family's Swedish meatballs
were not served in the 'standard'
way that you may think of, when
you think of Swedish meatballs.
Ours were (and still are) served cold
with toothpicks, *sans* gravy –
instead, with 'green sauce' (jalapeno
– or green pepper – hot sauce) from
a bottle. (We have Uncle Roger to
thank for this wonderful – delicious
– forever tradition.)

Meditate

*"If you knew, as I do, the power
of giving, you would not let a single meal
pass without sharing some of it"*
(Buddha Siddhartha Gautama)

Something to chew on

What do your holidays look like
today? How would you like them to
look?

Mantles – *today's* tradition –
core – assuredness –
repetition – certainty – no
surprises – safety…

Chapter 12

New tradition

Contemplate

"Therefore, my beloved brethren, be ye stedfast, unmoveable, always abounding in the work of the Lord, forasmuch as ye know that your labour is not in vain in the Lord" (1* Corinthians 15:58)

Text annotation

*Our good and inspiring works here on earth (including the magic of tradition) are not ineffective just as our good works for God are not ineffective.

Traditions are things that I can count on to stay the same. There's great comfort in that. A feeling of a safe place. The known versus the unknown. An anchor. Something to look forward to, whatever the reason, occasion, or holiday. There's an importance to it – the sameness of it. A reverence. We've had traditions – we've lost traditions – we have traditions – and simultaneously we are still working out new traditions for ourselves.

Family traditions are a pretty personal thing, based on your family history, your own family's priorities and desires, and based on your budget too!

We figured out when our own kids were very young, that

some of our priorities (wishes) were
to set aside some special days to
spend together over their summer
vacations, and also having a festive
Thanksgiving and Christmas
together every year. We knew that
those were things that made all of
us happy, and we wanted to start
some of our very own yearly
traditions together.

When the kids were four,
we heard that an amusement park
that was in our state, *'Darien Lake
Amusement Park'*, had changed over
to a *'Six Flags Theme Park'*, complete
with *Looney Tunes* and *Batman*
characters. I remember when we
saw the commercials for it when it
was brand new, and after we had
decided to bring the kids there, how
choked up I would get (*ok, I cried*)

seeing the characters on the
commercial, *just out of my excitement
and joy for the kids.* (*I'd run to the
television set when I heard the music for
that commercial come on.*) We stayed in
one of the park's RV rentals for a
couple nights that first year, and
eventually worked our way up to
week-long trips in those same RVs
as the years progressed. The point I
want to make here is that we kept
our yearly family tradition of taking
time off and celebrating it (time)
together as a family. (As I look
back now at all of those years of
trips there together, I realize that
the parts that I consistently think
about and remember the most are
when we were watching the kids'
faces and reactions – not where we
were.)

Along the same lines, my favorite memories with the kids are times when they were young and we had a day together at home, just watching their favorite television show and playing with their favorite toys on the floor, or doing a little craft together – just the everyday ordinary moments that are so cherished and sacred.

As the kids started to get older, our summer trip destinations changed. We eventually ventured to Canada, to *African Lion Safari*, and to visit Toronto and Niagara Falls, and then Philadelphia and *Hershey Park*, finally landing on the Thousand Island area, and the Old Forge and Lake George areas, in the Adirondacks. The latter became our "new Darien Lake" for many summers!

This brings us to the year that the kids graduated from high school, in which we decided to save up and splurge on a memorable trip to *Disney World* before they went off to college later in the year. (I'll admit it, we're still currently in a love affair with Mickey. For the record, *Disney World* IS one of the happiest places on earth – if for the feels from the Disney music alone.) Again, the best parts of all of it were the parts when we were watching each others' faces, reactions, and emotions, regardless of where we were –… having a special coffee with my husband on a bench in the Florida sun, the blue sky and palm trees overhead, watching our adult kids running to get back in line for a ride, laughing and hugging…

The joy is found in each other – no matter where you are (and it doesn't need to be an overly expensive vacation – it's more about tradition, repetition, and priority).

There is something to be said for having something to look forward to. To count down to*. Big or small things.

It's not where we went on our summer vacations, it's that we were together. We made memories together. That is something that is so precious, priceless, cherished to me. It will always have a very special and meaningful place in my heart. And we keep trying to make it happen together now that the kids are grown and live on their own,

even though most are staycations**
with everyone's busy lives and jobs
now. But it's still our tradition.
Their core. A form of assuredness.
Repetition. Certainty. No surprises.
Safety. (In this case in the sense of
routine and order). As I said, Jesus
became my core, and my husband
and my kids, my mantle. And we
want to be both things to them.

Another of our yearly
traditions is on Thanksgivings, we
adopted my mother-in-law's
tradition of making a trek to *Thanos*
and *Lombardis* (local Italian and
Greek import markets) for the
foods for our traditional Sicilian
Thanksgivings***. (We call our

Thanksgiving gathering with my husband's family, "Fake Thanksgiving" because we schedule it on a different day than actual Thanksgiving.) We used to celebrate our twins' birthdays at *Verona Beach State Park* every summer with their (paternal) aunts and uncles and cousins and grandparents, and one of our nieces once said, "*My favorite holidays are Verona Beach and Fake Thanksgiving.*"

Tradition = Connection

———————————

And when our children were toddlers, since we had many stops to make at our family's houses – which was a blessing of course –

over the course of Christmas Eve and Christmas Day, we started our own Christmas Eve EVE tradition. That day was reserved for just the four of us. We stayed home, enjoyed the tree, did our last-minute present wrapping, watched Christmas specials, ate, played, and just enjoyed *general leisurely Christmasing* amidst the excitement and anticipation of Christmas. And the biggest tradition of Christmas Eve EVE was our twins exchanging their gifts just to each other (still a tradition to this day). Lifelong tradition for a special lifelong twin bond and connection.

This is the reason tradition is so important to me. It keeps the bond and connection throughout the year – and throughout the years, no matter our distance apart.

Tradition closes the distance up.

It's the glue. And it also comes

back again to: a core. Assuredness.

Repetition. Certainty. No surprises.

Safety. We want to be their core

and their mantle through tradition

and all the rest.

Meditate

*"Greater still is the truth of
our connectedness"* (Buddha Siddhartha
Gautama)

Yes.

Text annotations

*Our favorite countdown now is to

put the next visit with the kids in
the books before they leave from
the current visit we're on with them.

**(some more of our favorite
beloved family daytrips): *Howe
Caverns, and then Iroquois Museum
down the street,… Aqua Zoo,
Rosamonde Gifford Zoo, Fort Rickey
Game Farm, and The Wild,… The
Lincklaen and Critz Farms,… Golden
Harvest Festival at Beaver Lake,… and
Verona Beach and Sylvan Beach
Amusement Park… and we continue to
discover new ones…*

***One example where I know that
smells = memories and tradition for our
own kids, is the presence in the
house of the treats and olives and
meats and cheeses that we bring
home from (our) Italian and Greek
import markets every year.

Something to chew on

What are Your traditions?
Is there anything you would like to
add to them?

Mantles – *today's* tradition –
core – assuredness –
repetition – certainty – no
surprises – safety…

Chapter 13

Trains

Contemplate

" *Whereas ye know not what shall be on the morrow. For what is your life? It is even a vapour, that appeareth for a little time, and then vanisheth away.*"
(James 4:14)

Train sounds are one of my favorite sounds on earth – especially at dawn and dusk, the only sound breaking the silence. The horn, the rumbling, and the powerful *swoosh* sound of the chugging on the tracks, the only other sounds in the air the distinct repetition of each of the unique birdsongs.

Part of the reason I love the sound of trains so much, and it is so comforting to me, is probably the familiarity – I grew up in a *train town*. And now as adults we live near several train tracks, so we hear the trains from our backyard.

Some more reasons that I just associate happy memories around trains is because my maternal grandfather had a great love of trains, and our kids also loved trains growing up. Our son had a cherished '*Thomas the Train*' set and also watched it on television, and due in large part to their love of trains, we started an annual Thanksgiving tradition of taking a train to Old Forge in the Adirondacks, on the day after Thanksgiving, to *Christmas On Main*

Street. Even the *train rides* to Old Forge are memories we hold close to our hearts — (*even the inevitable stress of just-the-getting-there-on-time — to the train — in the early morning.*) I always make us turkey and stuffing sandwiches for the train ride, from the leftover Thanksgiving dinner the day before. Once we arrive at the train station in Old Forge, we then take a bus to Main Street and start the morning with a breakfast or lunch *and our traditional special cocoa with whipped cream and sprinkles* at the local diner. Then the trek up and down the street to our favorite haunts. (All of the shops and even the street itself, all decorated for Christmas.) I just savor every bit of this day with our family — being present, and taking all of it in.

A few of our favorites
(along with the diner!), are: a shop
with narrow aisles – and aisles –
with shelves – and shelves of
collections, of knick-knacks of all
kinds, for all seasons; another shop
that sells rustic Adirondack themed
furniture, candles, toys, books, and
'dog-themed gifts'; a shop that has
homemade soaps; a shop that sells
antiques in the basement; the
'hippie store"; and last but definitely
not least, the *Old Forge General Store*,
which I think of as vintagey and
retro and has basically anything you
could think of. Throughout all of
these shops we all have our favorite
things that we traditionally look out
for, and the goal is also to do some
of our Christmas shopping for each
other here. One of my own

traditions, is that since the *Old Forge General Store* is usually our last stop before heading back home, I always stock up on an assortment of the old fashioned-stick-candy and bags of sugared hard candy to share for the train ride home, and then once on the bus to the train, and again on the train, we get off of our sore feet, sit back in our seats, try to get comfortable – and then we look around at each other, knowing that (although we're all exhausted – tired, sore, – *grumpy?*) we made another Thanksgiving memory! and enjoyed another stop together on our lifejourney.

Meditate

> *"You are far from the end of*

your journey "The way is not in the sky

"The way is in the heart "See how you

love" (Buddha Siddhartha Gautama)

Something to chew on

        What sounds – and what
"same-ness"   in   annual family
traditions – bring comfort to you?

Spirit nourishment

Contemplate

"And my people shall dwell in a peaceable habitation, and in sure dwellings, and in quiet resting places,"
(Isaiah 32:18)

In these chapters and seasons of my life, I am humbled and blessed to have been given a core and then a mantle – a safe place – a protective layer – arms to rest in – (people in my life who are my place of rest and safety and eternal joy). Assurance. (Tradition.) Constancy. Love. Care. Well-being. Peace. The known versus the unknown. These blessings Humble me and the realization of how blessed I am never escapes me. My heart also yearns for this kind of peace and tranquility and safe feeling for all human beings.

Meditate

"Then at last he is safe "He has shaken off sorrow "He is free" (Buddha Siddhartha Gautama – *the Dhammapada* 14:12 and 13)

Feeling safe had been my overriding need for my formative – childhood – teen years*. 'At last I am safe*. I have shaken off sorrow. I am free.'

Yes.

And just as in 'Jesus leaving the ninety nine to find the one', I have been able to experience and feel my own personal (triumphant) search and rescue operation (of that child) – of me**.

Text annotations

*simply my own feelings.
**('Takeaways for Sustenance'): My hope is that everyone who reads this and needs to hear this may be able to begin on a path of strength and healing, a feeling of safety, clarity and closure, light and joy. You don't need to keep shame/or be ashamed/or pretend that things didn't happen, either – (it happened). Or question how bad things were or if it was really

that bad – (it was really that bad).

Repressed memory, A Savior.
Until it isn't.
The Remembering, now the
Protector.
Survival. "Thriv-al".

Childhood trauma will markedly
change you and your demeanor.

However, your bright light –
your flame – will return.

Your beautiful humility
and compassion will remain
intact despite outside influences
and experiences.

I'm here to say that you
can acknowledge all of it and go on to

thrive and be happy.

You are a caretaker, a protector,
a lion or lioness you may have never had.

The pretense of the false fairy
tale and the lies don't matter and don't
deserve a place in your life.

Your worth is never
dependent on another's decision as to
whether you are worth enough.

Emotional neglect and/ or
trauma that you experienced as a child is
not a reflection of your worth.

Others do not dictate when
you do or don't matter, or when or whether
you are or aren't important in your place
in this world.

You are always important.

You always matter.

You are always worth so very
much.

You are always good enough.

You are always good.

You always have - and have
always had — all of the potential and
beauty and perfection that you should've
always been told that you have.

… Whether or not others are
proud of you, … whether they are deciding
whether you are good enough or true
enough, or deciding your worth, or talent,

*or importance in this world — in any given
day-to-day instance, as they please,… —*

None of that matters.

*Please Know and Believe that
your worth — and your sacredness — are
Never to be determined by another's idea
or belief or definition.*

*Finally, there Is Fruition in
Strength;*

*there Is Fruition in Steadfast
Fortitude;*

there Is Fruition in Hope;

and Dreams do come true.

You deserve all of it.

"The truth is always revolutionary." (Thomas Kennerly Wolfe Jr., 03/02/1930–05/14/2018, American author and journalist)

Text annotation

*(The preceding, all simply my own opinion.)

Part V The path: epiphany and enlightenment

Soul snacks (memory morsels)

Part V is a collection of anecdotal essays about a difficult season, followed by a path of fortitude, courage, strength, and healing, culminating in a lifejourney filled with many moments of Light and Joy. As always, it does not escape me, the great gift and blessing that these moments of epiphany, light, and joy are. I am forever grateful and absolutely forever humbled by it. *"Humble yourselves in the sight of the Lord, and he shall lift you up."* (James 4:10) *"Humble yourselves therefore under the mighty hand of God, that he may exalt you in due time."* (1Peter 5:6)

The following chapter (14) contains potentially triggering themes — and/or content — to childhood trauma survivors.

For M.C.M…

Fortitude – growth – self-
worth – self-love –
transformation – and grace…

Chapter 14

Shift

Contemplate

"What man of you, having (a) hundred sheep, if he lose(s) one of them, doth not leave the ninety and nine in the wilderness, and go after that which is lost, until he find(s) it? "And when he hath found it, he layeth it on his shoulders, rejoicing "And when he cometh home, he calleth together his friends and (neighbors), saying unto them, 'Rejoice with me; for I have found my sheep which was lost"
(Luke 15:4-6)

Hope

I was always — and still am

– a bookworm. I always loved
reading and I loved 'English' class
in school. I loved algebra – *I almost
think I would enjoy a basic algebra
workbook as much as a crossword puzzle
book for fun > (*shrugs shoulders* weird
I know, but probably true).* I loved
French class so much that I took
four years of it. I probably had the
potential of going through all of my
years in school as an A student, and
then going on to college, but none
of that would come to be. I was
simply 'surviving on
hypervigilance*', and even after I
was '*free from the earlier
circumstances** of my life', I still had
all I could do to function and
simply graduate high school, 'on
fumes'. To go back further, I'm
guessing that my demeanor, or

affect, – appearance (painful
shyness, intense sadness, fear*,
distrust, and social awkwardness) –
in elementary school made me look
uninterested in schoolwork (which
didn't help my elementary school –
or middle school – experience). In
reality, deep down I really just
wanted to devour the schoolbooks
and lessons and homework.
Instead, I was just on hyperalert*
and trying to be invisible – it took
up all of my time and energy – [due
in large part to the overpowering
shame and sadness I felt, without
knowing what to call it – shame that
didn't belong to me* – and also the
overshadowing (fear) of what the
day ahead would bring*]. And even
though it felt like 'shame', I feel it is
more accurate to call it

embarrassment. Emotional hurt*.
Mental injury*. (I also always felt
that my demeanor by force of
circumstance caused the teachers at
that time to hold me back from my
true potential and ability in the
classroom as well.)

I was in such a protective
mindset, that by the time I reached
middle school, my hygiene was
neglected and I slept in the same
clothes that I wore during the day
– for Days (layers of heavy sweaters
– in order to be shapeless –
overlooked – the layers of clothes
soiled from sweat. I stunk).
Keeping my armor around me so as
not to let my *self* ever be
vulnerable.

Since I mostly kept to
myself, I would roller skate or ride

my bike alone, and I also used to
love to take my tennis racket and
tennis ball and walk up to my old
elementary school where there was
a brick building – and hit the tennis
ball against the wall (in much the
same vein as using a tennis
backboard). There was a path –
made into a path from walking and
biking on it repetitively, by everyone
over the years – that went between
a few houses on my childhood
street (which we called – and still
call – "*the path*"), then a main road
to cross, and then the bottom of the
schoolyard. I can't help but see the
metaphor of: 'the path' – (to finally
hope, freedom?).

Marga (a Sanskrit term):
path to cessation of suffering.

⚬ ⚬ ⚬

213

Healing

I discovered makeup in ninth grade. There was someone on the television show *Donahue* demonstrating how to apply eye makeup – I watched it and tried it and ran with it from that day on. It got to where I would not let myself be seen without makeup – I would get up at the crack of dawn to start putting it on. I was honestly trying to hide my ugliness. I now know that I wasn't ugly – I was ashamed so I was hiding. And I now know that the shame didn't belong to me. (And I know that Mady is smiling because '*I do love me* and '*I know that I am beautiful*'.)

There was a cheerleading

tryout that year that I signed up for.
I was in line waiting for my turn,
then left the auditorium right before
it started. I couldn't articulate my
feelings then, but at that moment in
time I believe I thought I wasn't
worthy and mostly I just wanted to
remain invisible. I was incapable of
being social, from being – or feeling
– isolated* and alone for so long.
And the shame. I was lost. (*When I
think of it now, I wish I could go back
and mother this ninth grader – and all the
way back to toddler age really ... but in a
sense that's what I'm doing now.*)

    I ran from relationships –
friendships of any kind – before
they got too invested. I believe that
I came across as "stuck-up" to
some, in light of my demeanor...
and the façade that was my life to

the outside world… but it wasn't
that at all. It was the misplaced
shame. Sadness. Embarrassment.
Feelings of unworthiness. I ran
from school itself, missing most of
eleventh grade. I was running from
myself, and from feeling anything. I
remember sitting at a table in the
high school library with two girls
who were a little older than me. I
don't recall the entire scenario or
conversation but I do remember
one of them saying, *"I don't have any
problems."* I was stunned by that
sentence. As for myself, all I *knew*,
was being in a constant state of
fear*, feeling sadness, feeling
unsafe*, weak, unprotected*,
(unworthy), so what she said made
me feel confused, jealous, very
stressed, and I remember thinking

(about what she had just said):
"Wow. That's who I want to be." I just
wanted to sit there a bit longer — maybe
thinking I would pick something up —
some piece of information that I didn't
have, so I could have that too.

  I don't know exactly when
I realized that my normal was different
than other peoples' normal. — I think,
now, that everything from my
formative — childhood — teen years
can be looked at as
incomprehensible.
Incomprehensible, that behaviors
weren't able to be talked
about — taboo.
Incomprehensible — an
abomination, a horror —
abhorrent really, — to have
gone through what I had*.
Incomprehensible — that

no-one – not even those close to us

hears our silent screams when they

look in our eyes, or if they do it is

(*incomprehensibly*) with apathy, and is

not acknowledged or acted on.

Incomprehensible, that our minds

protect us by repressing our

memory. And that in a child's

mind, just having a place to call a

home and a family unit of any kind

overrides every other need

including the need to reach out to

someone or to run away from it*.

*"He giveth power to the faint; and to them
that have no might he increaseth strength"*

(Isaiah 40:29)

After I graduated high

school, drinking equaled numbing

which equaled freedom. Of course
I know now that what numbing
really equals is a path that has the
potential to lead to self-
destructiveness.

Repressed memory, A Savior.
Until it isn't.
The Remembering, now the
Protector**.
Survival. "Thriv-al".

Transformation

But my real freedom came when I
let myself know and acknowledge
and feel my (emotional) pain. Only
then was I able to begin to heal and
move past it – through it – and then
know joy. One of the most
important ways I was able to

achieve this was by not numbing my feelings related to my formative – childhood – teen years in life, with alcohol, quite honestly. I've just surpassed the two year mark since I made the decision to go 100% alcohol-free and I'm still smiling about it. Life is SO much better without it. I'm just so happy. I'm now able to live fully in my truth and even though my walk can be (emotionally, mentally) a painful one on some days (and never for missing alcohol), I am now spiritually and physically clear, awake, at peace, happy, present, blessed, and grateful, even on hard days. I behaved very socially awkwardly for many years to come – very cringeworthily immature***. Once I learned to put away the need to people-please, to be liked by everyone, – (inauthenticity, aka my survival mode) – my next lesson was that being authentic equaled being awake equaled joy. Being authentic also equaled being brave which equaled joy. Lightness. Freedom. (So much better than burying truth – carrying the weight of secrets that you shouldn't have to.)

We have shifts in maturity, shifts in priority, shifts in perspective. The former two, I feel, being more of a natural progression of things, the latter being more like an epiphany – a wondrous gift – and shift – of insight.

Freedom can also come by way of bravery. I never learned how to drive until I met my

husband. He took me driving, to
teach me, immediately after I met
him. I know now that he valued the
importance of (my) independence
and confidence – neither of which I
had up until then.

I thought there would be
no better feeling than the
independence (of knowing how to
drive), – and independence is very
important… but *confidence – oh wow.*
It's an amazing feeling. Life-giving.
I remember having driving dreams
before I learned how. Just driving
down the street 'like it was
something I did in real life, too'.

It's hard now to remember
a time that I didn't drive. And the
feeling continues to get even better
after teaching myself to back into
any parking spot like it is second

nature. I always used to look for
'pull-through' parking spots – up
until about six months ago. I just
kept trying and trying until I figured
it out. The point here: I don't even
know the moment I 'got' it, and
now it is so 'old hat', *but I really want
to hold on to the feeling of awe. (disbelief).
gratitude. (pride). confidence. An act of
self-care and self-love.* I know it's a
seemingly small thing – it sounds
silly – to be so emotional about
being able to back into a parking
spot but I really am still in awe
about it. The old adage, 'It's never
too late to begin' bears repeating.
*"God's grace and mercy are (brand) new
every single day." (Lamentations 3:22-
23)*

Rebirth

As I'm writing this part, we are on the cusp of Winter and Spring. There are always a few false-starts, but there comes that day, that you step outside and you say to yourself, *"It's here"*… I step outside into the light, look up and Breathe it all in. The sun shining Lighter – Yellow-er… God art… imitating… life. A waft of wet earth. A lilac scented breeze. The clamor of the seagulls – and the birds – *once camouflaged – now visible, all talking at once.* It's a whole feeling – not just weather-wise, but emotionally too. I find myself pausing to think to myself, *"I just feel happy right now."* The shifts in season always make me feel so alive,

* * *

so ambitious, so happy, so hopeful.
My heart beats faster. My nesting
kicks in. On these days, life looks
like a miracle and feels like love.
These are my days now.

Nirodha (a Sanskrit term):
cessation of suffering

*"…I'll tell you the best thing I
ever did do, I laid off the old coat and put
on the new,…"* (F. Graham 1859–
1931, 'I Laid Off The Old Coat
And Put On The New', 1914)

Meditate

*"You cannot travel the
path until you have become the
path itself."** (Buddha

Siddhartha Gautama)

*Clear the fear and the
unreasonable thoughts from your
mind, on the way to enlightenment,
epiphany, awareness, joy.

A few years ago, I wrote
down *"Perspective perspective perspective"*
on a piece of paper. I wanted a
reminder for myself to always take a
minute; to take a step back; and get
some perspective, especially when I
think I'm having a frustrating
moment or a bad day, and say *'Wait
wait wait — look at all that I have — all
that I'm grateful for — all of the blessings'*.
Yes, of course our feelings are valid
when we're having a bad day. But I
just want to remind myself not to sit

in it and make my home there. Is it
that those who go through the
hardest times have the strongest
faith or is it that those who have the
strongest faith go through the
hardest times? The former makes
perfect sense; – if you have faith
then you know. When it seems the
*center cannot hold (William Butler Yeats,
1919)*, your inner strength – inner
fire – hope – and faith – keeps you
moving, helps you to survive – and
ultimately, to thrive. The latter
probably translates as the ability to
stay strong – *because* of your faith
and beliefs. My need to be
hypervigilant – hyperalert – in
younger years, subsequently –
interestingly – ironically – carried
over to traits of being very
observant and aware, and quick on

my feet as an adult (quick to come
up with a solution whether it is to
solve a problem at hand or for self-
preservation)*.

Text annotations

*simply my own memories, my
own opinions, inferences, feelings.
**When I say Protector – what I
mean to say here is that not only
have I become a protector of myself
but more than that, ineffably, of my
family. **FEROCIOUSLY**.
***[actually, looking back on my life
now as an adult, I know now that
my awkward, (sometimes mean},
cringeworthy, immature social
interactions go all the way back to
my time in elementary school, and
although it is of my opinion that my

social behavior as a child was a direct result of my childhood traumas, I truly and with my whole heart apologize here for pain I inflicted through my (unknowing at the time, as a child) hurtful words – (*acting out*).] I think we should all feel safe in our own skin – in our own space – to say these things to each other – to genuinely apologize… to acknowledge… to hold space. And *Forgive yourself. Forgive yourself for being immature in the past. For placing too much importance on ego in the past. For past behaviors that you have outgrown and learned better by awareness, your watersheds. FORGIVE your LOW POINTS. Forgive yourself as you do better, as you move forward. "He hath shewed thee, O man, what is good; and what doth the Lord require of*

thee, but to do justly, and to love mercy,
and to walk humbly with thy God?"
(Micah 6:8) Show humility – in
giving and seeking forgiveness – but
just as importantly, forgive.
yourself. Show. Yourself. Grace.

Forgive yourself.

as you do better,

as you move forward.

––––––––––––––––––––

Takeaways for Sustenance

Last night I was watching a
journalist that I like, on tv, – and I
literally had to take a second to look
up a few words that he used, that I

didn't know the meanings of. And that's ok. It's great. I actually love it because I love hearing – discovering – new words. I had mentioned that my favorite subject in school was 'English' – (*reading*). We should use more of the words. I love the words. We probably only regularly use a miniscule amount of the words in the English dictionary. I have a physical dictionary and a physical thesaurus on my nightstand and on my endtable, to use when I'm reading or watching television or writing. Of course you can use an internet search engine – I do that too. But mostly I'm a 'physical book' girl. To delve even farther, there are all kinds of 'dictionaries' out there to explore that list unique, out of the ordinary, no longer used, or 'lost' words. I could go on about the love of words but just think of the power of words this way: Have you ever read a sentence with just a few words – but the *exact right words put together?* – and thought WOW, Whoa that's powerful, profound.

Something to chew on

Do you know how *beautiful* and *amazing* and *strong* you are? — how very *cherished*, *treasured*, and *loved?* — how *important*, *smart*, and *worthy?* Have You experienced any noticeable Shifts in your perceptions and thoughts and actions that have had an effect on Your life?

The following chapter (15) contains potentially triggering themes — and/or content — to childhood trauma survivors.

Growth – self-worth – self-
love – and transformation…

Chapter 15

Organic joy

Contemplate

"Now the Lord of peace himself give you peace always by all means "The Lord be with you all" (2 Thessalonians 3:16)

I have seen the term "glimmers" recently – everywhere. And I love it. Glimmers are described as *"tiny micro-moments of joy(,) that allow us to feel calm(,) and give us a sense of inner peace"* (Deb Dana, LCSW, psychotherapist and author)

Once, I felt what was unmistakeably a glimmer (before

that term had even come into
existence) when I was a teenager
just out of high school. I was home
alone in our pool, floating on my
back, looking up at a clear deep blue
summer sky, and the song that
came on, on my transistor radio,
was '*Top Of The World*' (1972)
(Karen Carpenter 1950-1983). It
was one of those rare moments
then, of feeling at peace, and it's
kind of remarkable that I have such
a vivid memory of that moment, –
that feeling!, – from over forty years
ago! It tells you how impactful
glimmers are! (And maybe the
impact of the proximity to water for
me)…. A marked sense of well-
being. Perhaps a *glimmer of hope,*
then, unknowingly? ('My music'
was my comfort. As a young

teenager in the early seventies, not
only did I rarely go anywhere
without my little silver transistor
radio in tow, I also kept it on, under
my pillow at night. That might
explain how I still know the words
to all the seventies songs.)

I now feel glimmers when I
first awaken in the morning – (I call
these glimmers my morning
glories!).

I also regularly feel them
when gazing out at our poplars on a
sunny day, – *my "church"*! Or seeing
a stream of sunlight coming in
through the curtain. It's no
surprise that the recurring theme
with (my) glimmers is sunlight. I
Need light in my life. In the literal
sense. If I had my way I would
have every light on in every room

all the time. Light light light.

Of late, the glimmers I experience in the mornings are very much attributed to being 100% alcohol-free for over two years now. When I started calling my mornings, 'my morning glories', I found faux morning glory vines and hung them with twinkle lights around the tall bookcases in our living room, as a reminder to how beautiful an alcohol-free life (and morning) feels and is.

Illumination

I finally opened my eyes to the fact that although I didn't drink every day by any means, whenever I *did* drink, I had no off switch. Binge to blackout. And when I

took a minute to look back over my
whole life up to now, lo and behold,
it had Always been that way. (I
couldn't see it at the time.)   In
instance after instance after instance
that I reviewed in my head, on the
sporadic occasions that I did drink,
No off switch. I just never had the
clarity before now or had opened
my eyes or had the aha moment
that this was the case. So I made a
lifestyle change – a healthy choice –
and a lifesaving choice I'm sure – to
be alcohol-free, over two years ago.
It felt similar to decisions to quit
smoking or stop dyeing my hair
years ago – I just woke up literally
and figuratively and knew that I
didn't want to do it anymore – and
in this case I finally had the
illumination – light bulb moment –

that there was an issue – a potential problem. Not to mention the argument of heredity. (Full disclosure: it took me three tries.)

Present day illumination

I'm healthier, really joy-filled (I call it organic joy), present, awake to everything, introspective, reflective, spiritual, grateful, and humble. Joy upon opening my eyes in the morning – even waking up and sometimes immediately smiling … just thinking about what this new day ahead holds – the weather – the day's plans – the people – and being fully awake – fully here – to all of it.

Stopping to appreciate everyday beauty in fellow humans is another take-your-breath-away kind of glimmer. …Just a few examples of this are some videos I have seen on social media that involve impulsive and raw beauty between strangers. One example was of three strangers singing together, impromptu on a subway platform, – and another, was of two strangers singing together in an impromptu moment in a grocery store. Another example is the trend on social media of "drive-by compliments" to perfect strangers. Beautiful human connection. Sacred in the everyday. Love. Life. Beauty.

————————————

The one thing that I never ever
want to take for granted or forget is the
sense of peace and safety! that I have in my
adult life, in my every day. Every. day.
Everywhere. All day. Free to be
'unguarded' – to just hang loose in my
own house and be me. Safely. Safe in my
own skin – no worries, no fears, no
hypervigilance! Constancy. Assuredness.
(I know, it sounds like such a seemingly
unremarkable thing, and it should be, and
it is, except for when it isn't.)
*(*Preceding paragraph simply based on my*
own memories and feelings.)

————————————

I leaned on Jesus and prayer
and I found my family – my safe

place, to get to this point. Family is about Trust, Care, and Safekeeping. A safe net. Find your family. Who is your family? – who fits into these descriptions? I know this is an obvious thing to say: family is most certainly your blood-related family, however it is not solely going to be the people who you are blood-related to. It's so much more than that too. Find your tribe who you love hard. Find your tribe who loves you hard.

Meditate

"You don't have a Soul "You are a soul "You have a body" (Buddha Siddhartha Gautama)

The DEPTHS of a traumatic childhood are not only filled with fear, indignity, and hypervigilance, but are sometimes also pervaded with a symptom wrought of circumstance, which is bedwetting — a day-to-day part of this type of childhood (and sometimes into teen years). And to be able to escape that — and escape the (misplaced) shame of that, too, and leave that in the past is also a gift of tremendous awe and gratitude.

*(*Preceding paragraph simply based on my own memories, beliefs, feelings, and opinion.)*

Something to chew on

How is your self-care?

For Cheryl…

Grace…

Chapter 16

Imprints

Contemplate

"Being confident of this very thing, that he which hath begun a good work in you will perform it until the day of Jesus Christ: even as it is meet for me to think this of you all, because I have you in my heart; inasmuch as both in my bonds, and in the defence and confirmation of the gospel, ye all are partakers of my grace"* (Philippians 1:6-7)

Text annotation

*agreeable; proper.

Over time, you absorb and adopt ways of doing things, and ways of speaking, from the people that you are exposed to on a daily basis.

One example is that I adopted a cousin's way of decorating her house for each season and holiday – (more of a sister and best friend than a cousin). It's not just the decorations themselves, but the feeling that envelops you that I love.

Decorating has become one of my all-time favorite pastimes, and hobbies. My very first exposure to this idea of *all-out decorating* the house came from my maternal grandmother, Mady, and my aunt (Mady's daughter, and also my Godmother). Mady's house at

Christmas lit Me up. – every. nook. and cranny. decorated. – attention to every detail with loving care, by Mady and my aunt's family. I remember the joy that it brought me, and it has stuck with me permanently. I still put in an honest effort to keep carrying on this tradition in my family.

I paid attention to – and still really *strive* to emulate this. It has had an impact on me and stayed with me, along with the feeling it gives me. Even just the *striving* of this in our house and in our day-to-day lives is so joyful. We can wake up and be new and start new always. *God's Grace and Mercy are new every single morning. "It is of the LORD's mercies that we are not consumed, because his compassions fail not*

"They are new every morning: great is thy faithfulness "The LORD is my portion, saith my soul; therefore will I hope in him" (Lamentations 3:22-24)

———————————————

Sometimes, we also adopt some of the beautiful things that we hear people say, as we go along on our journey in life, because it touches us, so we choose to say these beautiful words outwardly too. *A past co-worker of mine would always look you in the eye and hold space with you momentarily, to say "Thank you so much" whenever she would say thank you,* and that is something that I choose as my own phrasing and mannerism now, as well. Such a seemingly little thing! One of our

cousins always says, "*You're
beautiful*". It's a very impactful thing
to say to someone. I never miss an
opportunity now to say to someone,
"*You're beautiful*," or "*I appreciate
you*". Something else that has left a
lasting imprint on me is that I've
had people take both of my hands
in theirs, upon our introduction to
each other. That has given me
courage to also be authentically
myself (that it is ok to 'feel what I
feel' *and to Express it — Speak it).* It
comes back again to holding space
for someone. I like speaking what I
feel … telling a stranger that they
are beautiful … thanking every
service member I see for their
service.… An extended relative
looked me in the eye at one family
gathering and took my hands in his

and said, "*I see you*," and hugged me.
He very sweetly proceeded to tell
me that he saw *me*, my soul, who I
am. It really touched me. It still
does. It's not always our nature to
blurt out our feelings as soon as we
feel them – but it can really affect
someone positively. Sometimes
more than we could imagine.

―――――――――

I was able to spend some
cherished times with an aunt and
uncle and cousins (paternal-side) at
their summer camp at *Henderson
Harbor* on *Lake Ontario*, as a kid.
One of the memories that makes
me smile out loud is of my uncle
enthusiastically saying, "*Good
Morning World!*" every morning. I

always remember him having this
big smile and big laugh! that filled a
room. He and my aunt definitely
had a big presence – they were
Beautiful and they were a Light!
(The following could also fit under
the chapters on '*Safekeeping*' earlier
in this book): I loved "being part of
their family" on those days. I
always felt accepted, loved, and …
well … safe. It was a concept that I
didn't understand or relate to but
*that I knew that I wanted**.

———————————

Another of my memories is
that my (paternal) grandfather
would get up very early in the
morning, ready to savor all that the
day ahead held, and having done so

he would also go to bed very early
at night. Whenever we would visit
him, as he would be heading to bed
for the night, he would stop at the
doorway and say, *"Good night all you
beautiful people "You take care of
yourself"*

And our Nonni, was not
only just a beautiful human inside
and out anyway, but she always
looked beautiful too – (always
impeccable") – every day. Once
when someone told her this, she
replied, *"Dress for the day"* – (*As in,*
every. day. no matter the day). Four
simple words but with so much
meaning: be present; enjoy, live in
– and appreciate – every moment

• • •

you are in. This *is* the moment. My
daughter seems to have
inadvertently inherited this
philosophy and gesture from
Nonni, as it is also a motto that she
lives by — (one of those cool
ancestor trait occurrences).

There are people who cross
our paths who simply just affect us
with their very aura — their very
being.

An extended family
member who I was very blessed to
know and spend time with had this
kind of specialness. She was on this
earth with us well into her nineties,
and not only lived a very long full
life, but also a fully absorbing life —

storied. She had traveled the world.
She loved to sing – she will forever
be our soprano to the *FIVE
GOLDEN RINGS chorus* of our
renditions of *A Partridge In A Pear
Tree* on Christmas Eves together**.
And I later learned, upon seeing her
framed paintings, that she was a
very talented artist and painter as
well. Conversations – and time
spent – with her was a gift.

———————————

In the beginning days of the
pandemic four years ago, in one of
the "grocery store rushes", as I was
in the checkout unloading my
groceries, I looked up and saw that
the woman behind me only had like
five or six things in her arms to pay

for. I said, "*I want you to go in front of me* "*Otherwise you'll be here for an hour waiting for me.*" She was so appreciative. But honestly I felt that it was really no big deal and totally the right thing to do. She was checking out and said "I'm sorry, "*Could you hand me one of those gift cards?*" I asked her which one she wanted and handed it to her. The clerk rang her stuff up, I kept unloading my cart, and then I heard the woman say, "*Here this is for you*" "*What??*" "*Really??*" I was so overwhelmed by this. I couldn't believe it. She said that it was because I was nice to her, and that she hasn't been seeing enough of that in recent days. I was so touched – I still am, today. I literally felt like crying –

especially after the craziness and nonsense – and stress – in the store. I felt this was an amazing act of kindness that I received, so humbling and beautiful. I kept the sleeve that the gift card came in. It is on my desk at work where I can see it, to remind me of that day and how that moment made me feel.

Meditate

"Live purely "Be quiet "Do your work with mastery "Like the moon, come out from behind the clouds! "Shine"
(Buddha Siddhartha Gautama)

Suggested reading: *'The Five People You Meet in Heaven'*, Mitch Albom, (2003)

Text annotations

*simply my own memory and
feelings.
**When gathering with my in-laws
and out-laws and extended family
on Christmas Eve, we would sing
Christmas carols *to help Santa find us.*

Something to chew on

Who has left an imprint on
you and what was their action or
trait that has stayed with you?

Spirit nourishment

Contemplate

The bible has passages throughout, on suffering. (Jesus literally says), "*We will have suffering in this world*" Suffering is said to help us to better ourselves and our lives – the cessation of our suffering can bring us to a place of strength, endurance, awareness, wisdom, blessings, redemption, mercy, and grace. Grief and joy can coexist.

Meditate

Buddha Siddhartha Gautama's teachings are truths of suffering as well, as taught in '*The*

Four Noble Truths'* – "the truth (that there is suffering), the truth of the cause of suffering, the truth of the end of suffering, and the truth of the path that leads to the end of suffering – (the path to the cessation of suffering)." I also believe from my own experience that simply being *on* the path that leads to the cessation of suffering is *also, in those moments, a cessation to suffering.*

Text annotation

*the essence of Buddha's teachings.

Part VI New narrative: perspective and awareness

Soul snacks (memory morsels)

Part VI is a collection of anecdotal essays about the freedom of self-expression, humility along with the importance of self-love and self-care, and the importance of service. *"But the wisdom that is from above is first pure, then peaceable, gentle, and easy to be intreated, full of mercy and good fruits, without partiality, and without hypocrisy"* (James 3:17)

Joy and thrival…

Chapter 17

Rebirth

Contemplate

"Rejoice evermore "Pray without ceasing "In every thing give thanks: for this is the will of God in Christ Jesus concerning you" (1 Thessalonians 5:16-18)

When I discovered – and from then on, loved – St. Joseph's Day*, I was also blessed in finding 'my people' – my kindred spirits – who loved and celebrated St. Joseph's Day with me every year, two of whom were co-workers. We would visit a local chapel on our lunchtime together, and there

• • •

was a beautiful statue of Mary as well as candles you could light for prayer intentions and a place to kneel and pray. (This was in the same cathedral where our twins' Confirmation ceremony took place – officiated by our Bishop.) Visiting this chapel regularly was such a source of joy and peace for me. I'm reminded of pilgrimages, and a book called *'Looking For Mary'* (by Beverly Donofrio) – one of my favorite books, and my introduction to, and reason for my fondness to the Our Lady of Guadalupe devotion to Mary**. Our twins' Confirmation Recognition Mass was on the night before Easter at our church, at a candlelight Easter Vigil Mass. That night remains one of the most meaningful and special memories I have. Add to that, that Lenten week is always a time of deep emotion and reflection for me anyway.

And Fall is another season of rebirth to me. September first is like 'my New Years Day'. Renew. Rewake. Rebirth. Regroup. Reflect. Restart. It always feels new. Fresh. Hopeful. Joyous. Breathing in and feeling these first days – hints – of Fall are so life-giving and joyous to me, hard to even put into words here.

Our annual local 'harvest festival' always falls on the second weekend of September. (The calendar says September, but the temperature outside always ends up being one of the hottest weekends of the year.) But even in the

stickiness and heat, I relish this day,
even just the drive there,
surrounded by trees, and then farm
fields of hay; comforting farm-
smells and our tradition of getting
in line upon arrival for an apple
donut and cider; walking leisurely
(excitedly) along the paths of gentle
grassy slopes lined with craft
vendors; and then finally, taking the
hayride through the woods,
dreaming of Fall days ahead. (The
impending shift of seasons is
palpable, even in the sticky heat –
the very air itself – the breeze – the
smell of the air – the way the trees
move – the sky!) It's the time of
year that I feel the most alive! The
most awake! The most excited!
The sound and smell of a fresh pot
of coffee brewing. Reading a

favorite seasonal country magazine.
Making lists. Comfort-food
cooking. Making sauce! My
cherished 'sea of orange'
everywhere. The smells of leaves.
apples. pumpkins. campfires. The
silver leaves on our poplars
shimmering, swishing, clapping in
the wind. Just the way the days feel
now – they affect me right to my
very soul. The clouds so dramatic –
dark grey, sharply outlined and
illuminated in buttery yellow
sunlight! The leaves – God art! –
taking your breath away at every
turn, on the trees and underfoot,
like a colorful Frame surrounding
you and your day.

Meditate

*"Every morning we are born
again "What we do today is what matters
most"* (Buddha Siddhartha Gautama)

Recommended reading: *'Looking for
Mary: (Or, the Blessed Mother and
Me)'*, Beverly Donofrio, (2001)

Text annotations

*There was a severe drought in
Sicily during the Middle Ages.
People prayed to St. Joseph to
bring them rain, and he interceded.
After a successful harvest, to show
their gratitude, Sicilians prepared a
meal to honor St. Joseph, and also
distributed food to the poor. This
became an annual tradition, along

* * *
273

with serving fava bean soup on St.
Joseph's Day, because it is thought
that the fava bean was the crop that
saved Sicily from starvation after St.
Joseph ended the drought. More
St. Joseph's Day traditions include
making zeppole – a traditional
pastry, as well as breads made into a
variety of shaped loaves, such as
crosses and staffs, and wearing red-
colored clothing because in Italy,
the color red commonly represents
celebration and good fortune.
**The Virgin Mary appeared in
Mexico in 1531, in the last of
several apparitions. Our Lady of
Guadalupe's image is associated
with motherhood, feminism, and
social justice.

Something to chew on

What time of year – what activities/outings – what is it that makes you feel most alive?

Joy and thrival...

Chapter 18
Anticipation

Contemplate

"Now (may) the God of hope fill you with all joy and peace in believing, that ye may abound in hope, through the power of the Holy Ghost" (Romans 15:13)

Anticipation, planning, and Hope are some of the very best parts of life! Whether for holidays, special occasions, family visits, or just the upcoming weekend at home. For me, there is nothing – nothing – like the anticipation of the kids coming home. Simpler notes of anticipation include the joy

of strategizing decorating plans for
around the house for the next
season, or planning meals that take
more time to make, or that are a
little more special, on the weekend,
or on a day off from work. It gives
a very happy and satisfied feeling,
knowing that there is a meal –
comfort-food – in the crockpot or
the oven, or sauce and meatballs on
simmer, lovingly, painstakingly put
together, for the end of a full and
busy day. It leaves me feeling
accomplished and joyful! Even just
the acts of the planning, and the
shopping for the ingredients, are
joyful. But my two favorite
examples of the joy of anticipation
and planning, are: always having
the next tentative date in the books
for a visit with our adult children!,

and – Thanksgiving – my favorite holiday, because it's all about the people and the tradition of food!, and also, you still have all of the anticipation and excitement in the air of all of the upcoming holidays! I live for all of the menu planning! and decorating!, the festivities and family, football, and tradition!, that comes with the anticipation of Thanksgiving.

Another seasonal shift that is so palpable to me is what I call the sweet spot that I *start* to feel right around Memorial weekend. I love certain things about this time of year – from making strawberry jam to farmstands to family cookouts to most of all, my immediate family's

birthdays … but at the same time,
while all of the hustle and bustle
and business and heat of summer is
happening, I am starting to mentally
plot and dream about everything
FALL – (more strategizing). It's
like my own little happy secret in
my head. I'm really not trying to
rush time. It's more that there's an
importance to me – such joy! –
from anticipation of things that I
know make me really happy. *"When
times are good, be happy."* (Ecclesiastes
7:14) and *"When happiness shows up,
always give it a comfortable seat"*
(Patrick Stewart, as Ebenezer
Scrooge in *'A Christmas Carol'*)

I am *enamored* with Fall and
I start getting *really* excited for the
sea of orange right after July 4th. I
look forward to decorating for Fall

and Christmas all year. I try(?) to hold out until August 1st to start sneaking some Fall decorations out. Although I feel like I do leave a little bit of Fall out all year. Being immersed in Everything Fall is always such an indescribable happy place for me; the change in the light of the days; the way the candles and twinkle lights illuminate a room in shades of warm yellow and orange; the textures and shapes; the smells; but mostly the colors and lights. The last four months of the year are just a Feast of warmth and well-being and coziness and joy for all of the senses, with August feeling (to me) like a *Pause* right before it all begins in full throttle. 'A' is for August, and in this case 'A' is also for Anticipation. I often say that 'if

I had my way, I'd have a Fall room
and a Christmas room all decorated
all year round'. (I noticed recently
that although not totally intentional,
the house is starting to morph in
that direction.) Our dining room is
red, so I do have some red and
green décor in there. Our kitchen is
becoming more and more orange
and black, and our bathroom is now
orange and white. We'll see where
all of this goes. *I'm optimistic.*

(As a sidenote: I have also
been hearing about more and more
people basically saying, *'to heck with
waiting until a certain month rolls back
around'* to decorate their world in
the way that makes them feel the
most joyful, and some in fact
leaving Fall or Christmas
decorations up year-round. And I

have to say, I'm not angry about it.
I'm 100% on board.

I love a decorated world,
but my true joy peaks when the nest
is full. That's really who I'm
decorating for.

Ironically, at the same time
that I am feeling like I am living in
the Autumn of my life right now, I
also feel the most alive at the start
of this shift of season. *"Three grand
essentials to happiness in this life are
something to do, something to love, and
something to hope for"* (Joseph
Addison, English essayist and poet,

05/01/1672–06/17/1719)

Meditate

"What you think, you become
"What you feel, you attract "What you
imagine, you create" (Buddha
Siddhartha Gautama)

Something to chew on

Do you make it a point to plan, and to always have something to look forward to in your day-to-day in life?

The following chapter (19) contains

potentially triggering themes — and/or

content — to childhood trauma survivors,

and there are an allusion to/and instances

of profanity in this chapter.

[Robert F. Kennedy (1925-1968)]: *"I'd like to serve."* (1964)

Insight – epiphanies – my

voice – and h*ow may I serve*…

Chapter 19
Time

Contemplate

"Then cometh Jesus with them unto a place called Gethsemane, and saith unto the disciples, Sit ye here, while I go and pray yonder "And he took with him Peter and the two sons of Zebedee, and began to be sorrowful and very heavy "Then saith he unto them, My soul is exceeding sorrowful, even unto death: tarry ye here, and watch with me" (Matthew 26:36-38)

There's always the '*before-it-happened*' and then the *after*.

When you sit and think about it, it's really pretty *freaky* – for

lack of a better word. That 'bubble'
of time that precedes life
experiences to come, experiences
known or unbeknownst to you.
One of our examples of the *known*
was the Christmas before our twins
graduated from college. I wanted to
stay 'in the bubble' of that year and
never have to start the upcoming
new year, because that would be the
year that they would be graduating
high school and then moving to
college. The pain I felt, of that
knowledge – as well as the reality of
it when it came to be – ran very
deep and I just wanted time to
stand still on that Christmas before.
I came across something I wrote
that next summer, as I tried to
express what I was feeling: *"The air
is still and quiet, but for our tall tree*

branches gently swishing and swaying. I look up now and see and hear the leaves shaking — dark and green — silver dollars — against the sky. Incandescent rays of sun outlining an obstructive grey cloud, some of the rays escaping, alighting luminously on the treetops, the leaves, and branches. The hints of a rainstorm heading our way, but still a recognition of peace and beauty amongst the gloominess. God-Art... imitating... life, as I look back into the living room and see my adult children enjoying the last days of summer together before leaving for college... Wishing I could stop time for a little while more — bottle up these moments of peace and gratitude and grace in profundity — knowing that I just need to stop and take it all in — and hold onto it for another minute."

An example of the *unknown*

was right before 9/11 happened
and then after. Innocent to all of
what's about to happen, and to how
you and the world will be affected –
not knowing – and then the
knowing. The after. And you –
and the world – are changed – are
different – forever after. And
another example of the *known* was
in early 2020, just days before the
pandemic officially became '*the
pandemic*', when we were *still innocent
to the fact of it being*, and my daughter
and I took a day trip on a bus to
New York City. She had a job
interview there and I took a
vacation day from work to go with
her for the day. It seemed like it
might be a lot for me – physically –
to do this trip, but I decided to
just go for it and live in this

moment with her. My lesson of
that day: you need to live your life,
live in the moment, say yes, because
your timeline is only so long and
what are you waiting for? We had a
wonderful day together – a lot of
walking notwithstanding (no pun
intended there). And then as timing
(the pandemic) would dictate – we
would be homebound for many
days (and months) afterward. We
were together. But had I not gone
on that day, I would have missed
out on some very precious
memories of our first – and still
only – time walking around NYC
alone together as mother and
daughter. We have since been there
as a family, since she now lives
there, but that one day in time –
that point on our timeline – is so

important to me.

Just the concept of time can
be pretty profound to really sit and
think about, in the grand scheme.
I'm very conscious of the minutes
now – realizing in real-time, that
there may be things that you are
wanting to do – and things that you
are waiting to do – changes that you
want to make – but the reality is
that this present moment we are in
Is the moment to be lived in – now.
This is it. Don't miss it. This
minute needs to be savored – it's
going to pass either way. So many
times the realization kind of hits me
– of my timeline – of all of our
timelines – and the awe and
profundity (and fragility) of that.
We sometimes go blindly day to day
– drive… work… drive… home, …

and I'll be in the car and notice
headstones as I am driving by a
cemetery and can't help thinking
that 'they — *these people* — were *here*,
and now they are not, and none of
the trivial shit matters anymore'.
That will be me someday and none.
of. the. trivial. shit. will. matter.
Start not letting it matter now.
Transcend above the trivial. Spend
the days soaking in the joys. Savor.
Notice. Take the vacation. Retire.
Love. Do. I think a lot about this
these days. It's like looking at
vintage photos of decades past —
the turn of the century — seeing
how different life was — how
different life looked; the sharp
surrealness — the bolt of realization
— that you are looking at still photos
or films of people from just a few

generations ago, who are now gone from this life. People living their everyday life (their everyday moments, all so important in that minute), so focused on that moment like we are right now. The days and years and decades go so fast – we're here and then we're not – we are but a glimpse on a timeline. This is why I feel it is so important to put our focus on being present.

Ironically, the world looks to open right up – wide open – for you in later years – [meaning, you start (awakening) – realizing – what your true passions and interests and likes are, and you're pursuing them more fervently, purposefully, (and hurriedly?)] You're making it happen now. And it occurs to you

* * *

that these interests — and the paths
to them, and the recipes to attain
them, have always been there, but
you waited until now to look into
them and pursue them. It's okay
though. The time is now. The time
is made up of the moments that are
in today. And I feel that every day
now, and that's good.

Sometimes the gift of time
just comes in a form of a present
that we give ourselves. Some days,
you need to give yourself an hour or
whatever you need, to just sit and
be. Quietude. To think or not think.
Mindlessly watch a favorite
television show, really concentrate
on a documentary in the peace and
quiet, or sit in silence looking out
the window at the trees. The latter
is my favorite. Something magical

* * *

seems to happen to my mind when I look at the sky and at the trees as they Touch the sky. The green against the blue … the big-and-bulky-bigger-than-life-billowy-white-clouds against the blue. I do my best thinking and reflecting in these moments. I find myself looking up a lot.

As I'm writing this, I am sitting on the steps of our back deck, as I so often do these days, while our puppy runs around in the yard. He will look up every so often to make sure I'm still there or to see if I'm watching him, as a child might. Even though I'm a 'homebody', I definitely feel the joy and importance of getting fresh air every day, a look at the sky, the trees, and as I sit here in the refreshing cool air of a late May day, the sun peeks out from behind the clouds and I feel the heat of it land on the seam of my back — for only a moment, surrounded by a cool breeze. Similar to organic joy, I feel organic peace, organic contentment, well-being, when I sit outside. And I feel energy. Replenished, awake, aware, enlightened. It's no coincidence that the word enlightened' contains the word 'light'. But I digress, — sometimes your body, mind, and/or spirit need some time. Give it to yourself. It's yours to breathe in. Time is breath. And time is soul food — there to nourish you when you need it.

Based on my own
experiences, *cptsd* has a lot of stress
fallout/trauma fallout*, sometimes
regarding the most seemingly
ordinary life tasks. When I feel
overwhelmed with the tasks in my
house, I list every little thing. No
task too 'little' to put on the list.
And then I cross off what I've
completed. I may only finish one
thing at that time, or I may move
on to another. Either way I feel so
accomplished for achieving a goal.
The tiniest goal. Realize that you
only have the allotment of energy
each day that you have – for various
reasons. When it runs out, it runs
out. (Really know this and plan
accordingly.) Make 'doing what you
can' enough. Some of my reasons
for a 'cap' on my energy are just the

usual effects of getting older, and I would also add here: *please don't confuse the word 'lazy' or the perception as such, with what is actually just being 'very out of breath'* from dealing with chronic pain*, from (what I believe to be) *cptsd*, trauma response*, and freeze response**. Again, remember, *'Time* (for yourself) *is breath'*. Be realistic with your goals and self-expectations, and please always be kind to yourself just as you are to others. *(There Is always Hope for everyone, there is Fruition in Steadfastness, and Dreams do come true.)*

Another way I have found of really alleviating my stress and anxiety levels can be summed up in

one word: early. Start things early.
Be early. Whether it is in regard to
being somewhere, or for cooking
for a special day, decorating for a
holiday, cleaning the house – any
type of 'presentation' whatsoever,
start early. *EARLY* early. I can't
stress the impact and importance of
that enough. (I myself am striving
although I am a work in progress.)
If you have a small allotment of
energy each day and you know it,
start earlier. This is a huge form of
self-kindness to You.

Peace and patience go hand
in hand with these moments of self-
nourishing. The inner peace part is
obvious. The outer peace, along

with patience, just as important. It
is a surprising gift of circumstance –
and of surprising importance – that
I have been given, 'to be able to
tune into non-reactiveness' in the
initial moment of finding outer
peace*. I rely on slow and steady
breathing, along with my trait of
non-reactiveness, in the initial
moment that I'm accessing both my
outer peace and my patience. A
slow and steady focus on deep
breathing.

Another '*gift*' of
detachment is having the ability – the
skill – of letting things that happen,
or things that other people say, go.
Tranquilly breathing through any of
it – keeping it separate from your
own peace. Whether it is stressful
traffic, something breaking,

something spilling, a comment we hear about (or perception we feel) about others' feelings for us, a "right-fighter", or an "interrupter". None of that is truly related at all to us personally – to our truth. Just say okay. Breathe in peace. And breathe out untroubledness. The best personal paradigm shift of all is to happily move on with your day with your inner and outer peace, breathing in and out, smiling, knowing that these disturbances do not truly affect or reflect you or your day or your own practice of peace and calm, at all, in any way. They are separate things from you. As an important aside, we should remember to hold others with eyes and hearts of compassion as well.

I have also realized the 'gift'

(the *balance*) which is where I may painfully lack in being reactive on the surface sometimes, where my own feelings are concerned, I have been given the gift of possessing a great amount of empathy and compassion** for others. I am really aware of the compassion that I carry inside of me, and really aware of many sorrows in this world that are so beyond comprehension. It starts with caring. And then you do what your strengths and abilities allow. I feel we must all care. And we must all take care of each other.

I'm an avid backyard birdwatcher. They're all out now

that (as I was writing this) we're well into the throes of Spring. As I was driving home yesterday, I was noticing the birds all flying every which way overhead. All different kinds, just all cohabiting the spaces together – going where they want – doing their own thing – living their life unbothered. Sharing all the birdfeeders. Sharing all the spaces. So many different birds together. No bird issues.

Just an observation.

———————————

"It is important to be kind, even if it is irresponsible." (To be) – *"damn sweet"*. *That's what I have been trying to tell you. There are plenty of times in life when you do the competent, responsible*

thing. But, every once in a while, we (just) need to be damn sweet. If we're lucky, we'll never have to regret it." [Ed Asner (1929–2021) as *Lou Grant* on *'The Mary Tyler Moore Show'* (1970–1977)]

Meditate

"The trouble is, you think you have time" (Buddha Siddhartha Gautama)

Text annotations

*There are many pieces to the fallout of childhood trauma. One is 'shutting down' – I am still working on this. Another is the absolute necessity to take time to rest, re-group, re-set, re-charge, ('recover')

after any social activity. And finally,
the disquiet (pun intended this time)
that is felt along with the presence
of outside noise, or especially
sudden loud noises. (The
preceding, simply my own
inference, opinion, and conclusion
based solely on my own memory
and experience.)
**('Takeaways for Sustenance'):
Compassion can be a tricky human
emotion. You wouldn't think so; –
you would think it is simply a
'necessary and humane' human
quality. Compassion becomes
confusing and cumbersome though
when it clouds your emotions in a
situation where it has become
necessary to completely physically
and emotionally isolate yourself
from a person who was someone

who was close to you – who you
trusted. It is very hard to separate
away all pieces of human
compassion and completely
emotionally isolate yourself from
this person. It is an emotional and
lonely and torturous mindf*** –
(unfair to even be here) – and it
takes some a lot of time to arrive at
the place of completely
EMOTIONALLY isolating from
that person, because our innate
human nature is to be
compassionate. empathic. kind. –
add to, the emotional confusion
when it's supposed to be a trusted
family member. It first takes great
emotional strength, fortitude of
mind, spirit, resolve, self-care, and
self-love – and then… the act of
emotionally isolating from, can

finally – will finally – and should finally, be arrived at – over time. Then, the peace of … simply … release. (See Author's Note Part I – *there needs to be a perfect mix and balance of fortitude and strength; survival and release; peace, thrival, and steadfast safekeeping; and finally, humility and compassion in the midst of trauma. All parts as important as the rest.*)

Something to chew on

Are you being present? Are
you noticing the sacred in the day-
to-day? Are you allowing yourself
time for rest? Are you giving the
gift of time to yourself – are you
giving of your time to others?

My voice and how *may I*

serve...

Chapter 20

Taking up too much space

Contemplate

"But they that wait upon the LORD shall renew their strength; they shall mount up with wings as eagles; they shall run, and not be weary; and they shall walk, and not faint" (Isaiah 40:31)

After my (maternal) grandmother died, my husband and I were asked if we would like my grandparents' hutch, since we had just moved into our new house. It came over from Sweden, where my great-grandparents came here from. I have many childhood memories of the hutch at my grandparents'

house. *Smells* or *scent = memories,*
and it 'smells like my grandparents'
house', still, when you open its glass
paned and wooden door. I
remember being a small child and
my grandmother letting me get the
'good Christmas dishes' out from
the bottom part. It's like part of me
now. We've got most of it filled
now with things our children have
made for us over the years. It is
big, but it could never take up too
much space.

I call myself a maximalist
with a minimalist footprint. In
other words, I reuse and recycle, I
purge, I thrift, but I'm also ok with
collecting what makes you happy!
Decorating your world! And yes,
purging is always cathartic as well,
when it's time for something to go.

You'll know when it's time to
purge.

When I was thinking about
this, my mind went to other ways
that we think something will take up
too much space, that is part of who
we are and is important, like our
personality or our voice. If your
path happens to be very illuminated
by the light you give off, don't ever
feel like you are too much or are
too much light. Be the light.
Please. Your light is so necessary
and beautiful. If you Speak *Light*
when you feel it, keep speaking it. I
don't care if it sounds 'corny'. Your
words will be appreciated. It's ok to
take up the space – to fill the space
right up – with your light. *Imagine
being the sunlight someone needs, to thrive.
(And you can also be your own witness –*

*your own sunlight — your own validation —
your own approval — your own affirmation
— your own alchemist. You can be a free
thinker — you can be a "free agent
thinker".)* One of my very favorite
bible verses is: "…*and what doth the
LORD require of thee, but to do justly,
and to love mercy, and to walk humbly
with thy God?*" (Micah 6:8) In other
words, even the smallest actions —
whatever one is capable of — can
make a difference to someone and
does matter. I have to believe that
it all helps. If you do nothing, then
nothing = nothing. If you can do even
a little, then you've started on the
course of helping someone. "*Open
thy mouth, judge righteously, and plead the
cause of the poor and needy*" (Proverbs
31:9) I *strive* every. day. to be the
best human I can be. To be better,

do better, act better, live better, love better. I have regrets and have made big – cringeworthy – mistakes and (cringeworthy) bad choices in behavior. And I am personally sorry for that with my whole heart. I am sorry first and foremost, and secondly I need to also acknowledge that I believe that these behaviors are attributed to my cptsd – childhood traumas. I am always evolving, growing, and learning.

Sometimes the braver the thing is, that you are speaking out about, the smaller your circle gets. Circles are going to change. Whether you're speaking out on a person's or a group's behalf or speaking out on your own behalf – (about something that happened to

you). Know that you've got a
whole generation's attention
though, hanging on to your every
word and action, and your words
and actions matter. *"Someone needs to
get angry enough,"* (1968, Robert F.
Kennedy) (1925-1968) *"Just before
you break through the sound barrier, the
cockpit shakes the most"* [U.S. *Air Force
Captain Charles E. "Chuck" Yeager,*
the first person to fly faster than the
speed of sound ('Mach 1')]

Meditate

*"Chaos is inherent in all
compounded things "Strive on with
diligence"* (Buddha Siddhartha
Gautama)

Something to chew on

What would you use *your voice* for? What are you making space for – what do you need to make space for?

Spirit nourishment

Contemplate

My lifejourney includes
stories of the people that give the
safe spaces to hold space with; of
the roots that ground me; and of
the branches that keep me; a path
that enlightens me; and freedom,
wisdom, epiphany, a voice, and still
at sixty years old, the daily discovery
and evolution which is becoming
my changing narrative.

*"Therefore all things whatsoever
ye would that men should do to you, do ye
even so to them: for this is the law and the
prophets"** (Matthew 7:12) (*Do
unto others as you would have

them do unto you.)

*"Rejoice with them that do
rejoice, and weep with them that weep"*
(Romans 12:15)

Meditate

Compassion, the wish to
free others from suffering, is an
important part of Buddhist
philosophy. *Abhaya* is a Sanskrit
word, meaning fearlessness. Giving
someone protection from fear is
one of the three major types of
giving, in Buddhist philosophy.

Yes!

And I love that my path has

led to a discovery of Buddhist
philosophy and being able to learn
from it and embrace it side by side
with the parts of my *Catholic faith*.
I'm so thankful for this path I am
so fortunate to be on and my wish
and my hope is for all to find their
roots, core, and mantle, and to walk
on a path of hope and "strival"*
and ultimately "thriv-al".

Text annotation

*"strival": the act of striving
towards.

Part VII Author's note part II,
epilogue, postscript,
acknowledgements, references,
about the author, and afterward

Author's note part II

Human acknowledgement,… and acknowledgement By humans,… will change your life.

Awareness… – and in turn… awe… , – of nature around you…, – of the sky…, of Light… – will change your life. All is connected.

Care… compassion… kindness... dignity… respect... and love... for Yourself… and for Others... will change your life.

Humility... gratitude... positivity... and faith... will change your life.

Sparks of faith – that turned into a strong faith – and sparks of strength – that turned into fortitude, courage, and toughness of spirit – brought me through tribulation and onto this healing, blessed, and beautiful path. My family and the people that I am blessed to have on this walk with me have kept – and keep – my spirit nourished and my soul safe on the journey.

Epilogue

I have always wanted to go on a religious pilgrimage.

It's tough sometimes to be able to travel, to go on one. A few of my family members have gone on them and one of my coworkers has gone on some as well. I feel myself absorbing their experiences – their feeling – as they recall their trips back to me. I'm feeling it now as I write this. It's definitely on my bucket list. Also on my bucket lists are to experience visiting churches that I have never been to… – experiencing a spiritual retreat(s)… – and to revisit my ancestral 'climb'! I suppose? I am searching for something? (unnamed – unknown!).

I have been so blessed with finding my way to a path of absolute peace – release – and love – so it's not that I'm missing something. I'm not. I do however continue to be hungry for more knowledge about my bloodlines (not only for myself but for my kids). (Even though I'll Always be a Swede in my heart.) I continue to be hungry for continuous learning about Jesus ministry and other spiritual philosophies – and the freedom to make my own choices about my own beliefs and practices as I continue on a path to awakening and enlightenment.

And finally, I continue to yearn to find ways for how I may serve. Have my formative – childhood – teen years led me on

a path to having the gift of wanting
to help others who can't help
themselves? Of being strong for
someone else? This is the path I am
now on – my intention. Things
have all turned out for me – my
walk has led me o a path to a
beautiful journey. I guess in a way I
have already been – and still am –
on a pilgrimage these sixty years.
But I'm always open to an epiphany
or spiritual awakening.

Postscript

Right as I was readying –
preparing – to publish this book, a
solar eclipse took place – and the
city where I live was within the
pathway where it was a viewable
event. I found that I had a lot of
thoughts about it – and about the
sky – that I wanted to write about,
thus my postscript. Before I get to
my thoughts on the eclipse, I would
like to reflect on the *'profundity of
grace' of the sky – and the clouds.*

Our son's college was a
three-hour drive away. It doesn't
sound like a lot, but it was, when it

came to driving for six hours for a
same-day round trip, or even just
the prospect of us meeting up for
dinner or for a visit – (and I always
miss my kids anyway). Once, on
the drive home after dropping him
back off at college, during one of
those infamous Upstate New York
winters that we have, I was feeling a
combination of nervous about the
driving conditions, and sad at
already missing our son. I was
praying quietly that my husband –
who was driving, and the roads, and
my son, would be ok, and I looked
out the car window and I saw a
wispy cloud in the form of an angel
– or maybe it was an angel.

    I love the *signs* (answers).

In another instance, – on
another afternoon, – I had gotten
word that my grandfather (my
Swedish grandpa) was moved to an
assisted-care living facility very close
to where we live. My response was
surprise and I planned to visit right
after work the next day. When I
got up for work the next morning, I
got a few phone calls from some
family members that my grandpa
had passed away early that morning.
I was sitting in the dark of our
living room and then out of the
corner of my eye I noticed a
battery-operated candle flicker on
for only a moment, then back out
(one of those little 'votive' button-
battery operated candles that had
long been in need of being switched
out for a fresh one). I couldn't get

it to turn on again. Then I stepped
out onto our back deck and looked
up to the sky to see the most
beautiful 'set of angel wings'
(cloud). I took a picture of it. I
keep it on my desk at work along
with a picture of the angel (cloud) I
saw on the way home from our
son's college. I say clouds – but –
(*shrugs shoulders*)…

———————————

Witnessing the eclipse event
was awesome. It ended up being
pretty cloudy here, but for me, the
cool part was the darkness falling
over, like nightfall in the middle of
the day, and then going back to
daytime. The temperature dropped
noticeably. The insects and birds

● ● ●

got quiet. It was an awe-filled,
profound, exciting, – kind of a
spiritual moment. Very communal
– all of us experiencing nature – and
God – from this planet, – waiting
together, as our moon aligned
perfectly with the sun and the earth,
paused – as if to acknowledge – and
to give us a moment to
acknowledge – the perfect
alignment of the universe – and
then continuing on its perfect path.

———————————

I'm forever staring at the
sky. And forever in awe of it. The
sunrises on my drive in to work
each morning. The sunsets from
our back deck, different with each
shift of seasons – wisps of pale pink

and yellow cotton candy in the
Spring; melting into one vibrant pile
of color in the summer; dramatic
amidst the sharpness of the dark
grey clouds, starkly outlined and
backlit in yellow, in the Fall; shades
of purple cotton candy in the
Winter. The clouds, their
appearance shifting with each
season too! And sunlight, always
immediately lifechangingly lifting
my spirits. I like to say that the
answer can always be found looking
up – the Wondrous feeling of
looking up to the sky – savoring the
moment and Breathing It All In –
my heart can hardly take in all the
joy of it. Healing, in the form of
'skying' perhaps? *Always look up.*

Postscript to my postscript

    I really do believe in miracles…
(Lazarus)…

Text annotation

*'skying', in the same vein as
'grounding' or 'earthing'.

Acknowledgements

It's near an impossible and truly
humble task to thank everyone
sufficiently and appropriately,
inclusively, but I did my best:

To Mike:
There's a quote I heard (unknown
source/credit) that says, "*sometimes
the only thing we can find time to do is to
quarrel,*" and we could jokingly say
that sometimes… but kidding aside,
more than anything else, you are my
mantle and my safe place, and I am
beyond grateful and humbled – in
my feeling of overwhelming
gratitude – for the greatest gift, of
being able to stand in my own
house, at any and every time of day,

every day, and feel peaceful – safe –
happy – worryfree.

To Mike, Hannah, Zachary, and
Victoria:

for the gift of being my family, my
blessings, my world, my heart, my
everything and for all of your
unconditional, enthusiastic,
passionate support, love, belief,
mentorship, and encouragement at
every step of this journey, for being
my mantle, for proofreading for me
(Hannah), and photographing my
back cover art (Zachary).

To all of my immediate Fitzgerald
and Koziara *and extended Fitzgerald
family – Eileen, Jim, Karie, Patty L.,
Kathy K., and Sunny)*/ and Scuderi/
Frank/ Barnum/ Lafrance/
Lagstrom/ Lavine/ and Morey
families:

for your excitement, enthusiasm,

and immediate and unquestioning

belief in my dream, and your

unconditional and beautiful family

love and bond.

To Grampa and Laura:

for being grandparents and for

always being there.

To all of my nieces and nephews

and spouses of nieces of nephews

who are also my nieces and nephews:

you are beautiful. I love you. And

the love that you give back to me is

beautiful and it is everything to me.

To Chrissy, Andre, TJ, Stasia,

Cheyenne, and Erik H.:

for your beautiful love, for letting

me always be your honorary Aunt,

for calling me Aunt, and being

cherished nieces and nephews who

I am endlessly proud of. You don't

know how much extra joy and light
you bring to my life.
To *all* of my coworkers:
for your friendship, encouragement,
mentoring, support, and patience
with me, and belief in my dream
and praise *that I am so humbled by*,
and special notes to A.Z. for
humbling me with your reaction
and praise, S.M., A.B., and E.A. for
endlessly listening, D.C., K.B., R.W.,
C.H., T.D., and T.G. for your
unconditional support, L.L.T. for
always being there, and J.McC:
for inspiring me of the importance
of sharing our life stories, through
the humbling gift of the beautiful
sharing to me of your own stories.
To Lisa L.–H.:
for the gift of rekindling our
childhood-neighborhood

friendship, for being a kindred spirit and sister as an adult, and my bookworm buddy.

To Lorraine, Kathy C., Jojo, Doug S.L., both Bill P.s, Frankie, Lauren C., Jim C., Paula S., Liisa, Carolyn S., Jim J., the Bill family, Lisa D., Betty and family, Christine D., Colleen P., Colleen G., Susan C.–S., Cindy B., Molly B., Angela K., Angela B., Lisa J., Deb B, Mark K., Jessica F., and Mau P.:
for being there.

To Julie and Sheryl:
for your immediate and unquestioning encouragement to proceed with my dream and for friendship and sistership and a shared constancy in faith.

To Venessa, Uncle Eric, Kimmie, Connie S., Doreen, and Janie:

• • •

for your unconditional love and
support and walking side by side
with me, our unbreakable and
cherished tie, and 'your hand in
mine', every day.
To *all of my out-laws, in-laws, and
extended families by marriage*:
for forever cherished family bonds
and family love.
To Betty and family, Lisa B.,
Jennifer L., Julie and Joey, Susan
and Stuart, Anne, Caryn, Francine
and Carmen and Carmen III,
Cheryl, Rick and Jean, John and
Carolyn and Edward and Uncle
Walt:
for cherished family ties,
and for your beautiful
cousinship and friendship.
I love you.
To my soulsisters, Sheryl,

* * *

Denise, Anne, Peg, Ann, Linda,
Donna, Mary Beth, Nela, and Sue:
for your immediate and unwavering
support, belief, pride, enthusiasm,
and excitement for me and for my
book. And for your gentle patience
of my hermitness and insecurities
while giving me the unbelievable
beautiful gift of having you for
soulsisters in this season of my life.
To BethAnne, Linda G., and
Kathleen L.:
for your inspiring, spirit-filled
positivity, your light, your
friendships, and your daily
encouraging words.
To Art:
for your mentorship and interest
from the beginning of my career
thirty-five long years ago, for your
continued friendship, and your

positivity, joy, and wonder of every day.

To *ALL* of my immediate and extended Family, in-laws, *out-laws*, and Friend-Family, lest I forget any one of 'my beloved'; to those who have passed on from this earth (my guardian angels); to those who are still walking the path here with me; and to those who have touched my heart and soul and are mentioned throughout these pages: for holding space, being a safe space, and being great teachers and cherished companions on my journey.

Finally, to the inspirers, the pavers, and the brave.

References

Batman is the property of DC Comics and used only for reference in my mention.
Looney Tunes is the property of Warner Bros. and used only for reference in my mention.
All bible verses are KJV (King James Version) are not under copyright and are attributed appropriately on applicable book pages.
All quotes from Buddha Siddhartha Gautama are not under copyright and are attributed appropriately on applicable book pages.
All other quotes and titles are used appropriately within Fair Use copyright act and are attributed

appropriately on applicable book pages.

All products are used only for mention and are used appropriately within Fair Use copyright act and are attributed appropriately on applicable book pages.

About the author

T. L. Fitzgerald is a mom of twins, a self-proclaimed *Jesus Freak,* and debut author at sixty years old. Along with her husband and family, and their and their children's furry family members, she currently calls New York home. Her family is her world, she currently works outside the home, and is looking forward to her next chapter which includes retirement, more family time, more holding space, more writing, and more home decorating. She is a vocal mental health advocate, a vocal advocate for safeguarding/safekeeping of children, elderly, and vulnerable or discriminated-against persons, and in her later years has evolved into a free thinker > *or "free agent thinker",* and a feminist. In retirement, in addition to the aforementioned, she has goals of becoming an end-of-life-doula and is looking forward to everything else the coming years have in store.

Afterward

It is sometimes something
of an *impossibility* to try to 'reconcile
one's *childhood*'. Or to understand
the mechanism of repressed
memory… In my case, there's been
no great epiphany or even a
meaning for good. I've finally
arrived at a stopping point of any
continuance of deep thoughts or
any types of comprehensive dives
of analysis on my part in regards to
it all. We can change our thoughts
– we have a *choice*. It's a battle that I
finally won. It was all too
emotionally-physically-mentally
taxing, and my goal now is not to
rehash (my childhood) but instead
to look for meaning in the everyday

of the *present* day. The sacred in this ordinary – the divine in *this everyday.* Now. Today. The profundity of *this.* The sacred of the timeline remaining. *These* epiphanies. *This* awe. The *gifts* of *this* chapter. Peace. *Release.* The beauty of these days is breath. The beauty of these days takes my breath *away.* *"It came to me that I should teach this truth for it is real happiness and joy "The cessation of suffering is possible"* (Siddhartha Gautauma Buddha)